PREACHING

JAMES

Preaching Classic Texts

Preaching Apocalyptic Texts
Larry Paul Jones and Jerry L. Sumney

Preaching 1 Corinthians 13
Susan K. Hedahl and Richard P. Carlson

Preaching Genesis 12–36
A. Carter Shelley

Preaching Hosea, Amos, and Micah
Charles L. Aaron Jr.

Preaching James
William R. Baker and Thomas D. Ellsworth

Preaching Job
John C. Holbert

Preaching Judges
Joseph R. Jeter, Jr.

Preaching Luke-Acts
Ronald J. Allen

Preaching Resurrection
O. Wesley Allen, Jr.

Preaching Romans
Bruce E. Shields

PREACHING

JAMES

WILLIAM R.
BAKER

THOMAS D.
ELLSWORTH

CHALICE
P R E S S

ST. LOUIS, MISSOURI

Bible quotations, unless otherwise noted, are from the *New Revised Standard
Version Bible,* copyright 1989, Division of Christian Education of the National
Council of the Churches of Christ in the United States of America. Used by
permission. All rights reserved.
Scripture quotations marked (NIV) are taken from the HOLY BIBLE, NEW
INTERNATIONAL VERSION®. NIV®. Copyright © 1973, 1978, 1984
by International Bible Society. Used by permission of Zondervan Publishing
House. All rights reserved.
Quotations marked (Message) are from *The Message* by Eugene H. Peterson,
copyright (c) 1993, 1994, 1995, 1996, 2000, 2001, 2002. Used by permission
of NavPress Publishing Group. All rights reserved.
"Death or Life in Words" on page 96 is from *Knight's Master Book of New
Illustrations* by Walter B. Knight (Grand Rapids: Eerdmans, 1973). Used by
permission of the publisher. All rights reserved.
Quote from Billy Graham column used on page 159 is used with the permis-
sion of the Billy Graham Evangelistic Association.

Cover art: Detail from stained glass, St. Lorenz, Nuremberg, Germany.
              Photograph © The Crosiers.
Cover design: Michael Foley/Elizabeth Wright
Interior design: Wynn Younker
Art Director: Michael Domínguez

Visit Chalice Press on the World Wide Web at
www.chalicepress.com

10 9 8 7 6 5 4 3 2   06 07 08 09 10 11

Library of Congress Cataloging–in–Publication Data
Baker, William R.
   Preaching James : preaching classic texts / William R. Baker, Thomas D.
Ellsworth.
       p. cm.
   ISBN-13: 978-0-827229-80-8
   ISBN-10: 0-827229-80-1 (pbk. : alk. paper)
   1. Bible. N.T. James–Commentaries. 2. Bible. N.T. James–Homiletical
use. I. Ellsworth, Thomas D. II. Title.
   BS2785.53.B35 2004
   227'.9107–dc22
                                                      2004005325
              Printed in the United States of America

CONTENTS

"Consider it pure joy…" JAMES 1:2 (NIV)

To Elsie, Emily, and Rebekah:
You have made the journey "pure joy."

THOMAS D. ELLSWORTH

My journey with the letter of James begins thirty years ago in the western suburbs of Chicago with the weekly gathering of "young adults," in association with the Hoffman Estates Christian Church, who met for Bible study in the tiny condominium my wife and I owned. The faith-deepening caused by this little book "in the back," and the energetic exchange of ideas from the group, propelled me to see James as ripe for academic research. Just a few years later, at the University of Aberdeen, Scotland, I would find myself knee-deep in James as the focus of my Ph.D. thesis, titled *Personal Speech-Ethics in the Epistle of James* (completed in 1986 and published by J. C. B. Mohr in 1995 in the WUNT series). Since then, in addition to presenting various research papers for academic gatherings, I published a guide to understanding James in the Standard Bible Series (Standard Publishing, 1990) and a popularization of my Ph.D. thesis, titled *Sticks and Stones: The Discipleship of Our Speech*, with InterVarsity Press (1996).

My fascination with the letter of James never seems to end. So, I am thankful to Chalice Press for giving me the opportunity to work through James yet again for their *Preaching Classic Texts* series. Thinking about providing exegetical information on James for preachers has improved my own understanding of James in the process.

One of the highlights of my years in St. Louis as Professor of New Testament, Saint Louis Christian College, was my long lunches with Jon Berquist–then senior academic editor for Chalice Press–at those odd little places in downtown St. Louis, talking about many things well beyond James. Thanks also to Susie Burgess, director of marketing at Chalice Press, who has really helped me feel at home with Chalice Press over the years and has been so supportive of the *Stone-Campbell Journal*, of which I have been general editor since it launched in 1998.

Jane McAvoy, editorial director at Chalice Press, graciously received this manuscript her first day on the job. She has been an invaluable source of much-needed help as the manuscript has headed to publication.

Since joining the faculty in 2002 as Professor of New Testament, Cincinnati Bible Seminary, I have greatly appreciated the encouragement I have been given to complete writing projects, especially the sabbatical provided at the beginning of my employment. It is this kind of understanding and generosity from the administration at CBS that makes it possible for books like this one to be written.

My special thanks goes to Tom Ellsworth (an alumnus of both Saint Louis Christian College, where I began this project, and Cincinnati Bible Seminary, where I completed it) for joining with me on this project. His experienced preaching for a thriving congregation of more than two thousand members gives the sample sermons credibility. Each sermon has clear insight and a wealth of illustrations, both of which young preachers as well as seasoned preachers will find helpful. Both of us encourage preachers and teachers to use the sermons or the exegesis in any way that seems most fitting. Note that I wrote the Introduction as well as all the exegesis sections, while Tom has provided the sermons.

WILLIAM R. BAKER

The letter of James is a favorite of mine. I like practicality, and James is a cut above when it comes to practical theology. He minces no words; each time I read through these five small chapters my Christian walk is challenged and humbled. His letter is also a great source for preaching; the message cuts across all social and economic lines, applying to every listener. The sermons contained in this book were developed from a series I preached in 2002 at Sherwood Oaks Christian Church, Bloomington, Indiana. I am indebted to this wonderful congregation who has listened, encouraged, and, at times, tolerated my preaching for the last twenty-three years. I have gained far more from this church and her leadership than I could give back in several lifetimes.

Thanks also to: my loving and caring parents, Tom and Midge Ellsworth, for teaching me the love of Jesus Christ through word and action; co-author Dr. William Baker for giving me the opportunity to join him in this exciting project; the faculty at St. Louis Christian College and Cincinnati Bible Seminary for giving me the tools and the heart for ministry; and Donna Pruet, my administrative assistant, for her gracious help with this project.

A special thanks to my wife, Elsie, and our daughters, Emily and Rebekah, for their tireless support. Their love, patience, and encouragement through the years have sustained me and have made coming home the best part of my day.

THOMAS D. ELLSWORTH

Orientation to James

James may be short, but the church testifies to the punch it packs. The punch comes because James talks about issues that matter to people today and every day. It speaks in a thoughtful, hard-hitting manner. New Testament scholars often question what James meant in its original context. The modern church ignores this historical gap, sensing the book's immediate, contemporary application in their lives.

Such immediate application comes when James deals with daily struggles in life: prayer, prejudice, God, sin, daily conversations, faith, anger, living out our faith, getting along with one another, repentance for insulting God with our selfish attitudes, unfair treatment by social superiors, the Lord's return, prayers for healing, and spiritual restoration.

Because people in the church love this book and turn to it often for their personal devotions, preachers find it a great book to adopt for a preaching series. This Chalice Press volume will help you do this well, providing both useful insights into the text and its historical background, and sample, expository sermons to serve as guides for your own efforts to enrich the lives of your congregation with the challenges of James's letter.

This overview of the letter will prepare you to deal with particular passages. No other New Testament book is associated with James, so we don't have nearly as much to go on as we do with a book such as Galatians or Romans, authored by Paul.

This makes it all the more important to digest the available information.

James comes out of a sphere of Near Eastern writing called wisdom literature. This kind of literature is most easily observed in the canonical books of Proverbs, Ecclesiastes, and Job, but also in the noncanonical books of Sirach and Wisdom of Solomon. This writing style dates back to the earliest writings of humanity in Egypt. This literature often takes the form of a father writing to his son, or a teacher writing to his students about what is really important in life, and detailing the keys to success. The purpose usually is to encourage the reader to be morally upright in habits and especially in speech. Proverbs and catchy sayings are liberally employed and passed on to the reader. Gaining wisdom, then, is about becoming more and more skilled in the daily routines and relationships of life.

The letter of James fits into this wisdom style of literature in a number of ways:

1. James 3:1 indicates the author is a teacher.

2. James 1:5 and 3:13–18 encourage the readers to become wise, and it is easy to read the entire book from this perspective.

3. James includes many proverbial sayings. Particularly noteworthy are the ones in James 2:13; 3:18; and 4:16, which function as memorable conclusions to significant teaching.

4. In a mere 108 verses James contains an astonishing 32 ethical imperatives. Many of these concern appropriate speech.

5. Maturity appears to be the unifying theme of James. It is best summarized in 1:4; 2:22; and 3:2. The author challenged his readers to grow in spiritual maturity. Such growth will be evident in their daily behavior and in their relationships.

Knowing that James is wisdom literature changes our expectations as we read it. We cannot look for the same patterns of communication or even the same theological concerns we are comfortable with in Paul's writings. Paul's highly logical, carefully argued and defended approach is much more akin to modern, Western writing patterns. James's way of thinking is much more Eastern. Even today oriental speaking and writing reflect the same concerns about wisdom, and even the same free-flowing pattern of communication. When we feel like James seems disorganized and not tightly argued, we are projecting our Western bias on it. The logical links between sections of James may not be spelled out. This forces us to take a step or two back from the text to discover such links implanted in the association of words and ideas. Approached in this way, James demonstrates a richness that is striking, powerful, and persuasive.

The author uses creative techniques to hook units of thought together. One such technique uses a word both at the close of an opening unit and at the beginning of the second unit. This occurs most obviously in the first chapter, when the word "endurance" hooks 1:3 and 1:4, "lacking" hooks 1:4 and 1:5, "temptation/tempted" hooks 1:12 and 1:13, "gives birth/gave us birth" hooks 1:15 and 1:18, and "religion" hooks 1:26 and 1:27.

Another technique helps the author build cohesiveness. This involves coming back repeatedly to subjects introduced earlier: God's protection of the poor and general disdain for the rich (1:9–11; 2:5–7; 5:1–6); prayer (1:5–8; 4:1–3; 5:13–18); personal speech-ethics (1:19, 26; 2:12; 3:1–13; 4:1–3, 11–12; 5:9, 12). One alternative suggestion for preaching James, as opposed to the section-by-section exposition we will do in this volume, is to preach these subject-related sections as units of one sermon.

Having learned to read James as Eastern wisdom literature, we must then become aware of the Jewish and Greek cultural influences embedded in the letter. On the Jewish side, James contains numerous Old Testament quotations (Lev. 19:18 in 2:8; Ex. 20:13 and Deut. 5:17–18 in 2:11; Gen. 15:6 in 2:23; and Prov. 3:34 in 4:6). Other passages appeal to four Old Testament personalities (Abraham in 2:21–23; Rahab in 2:25; Job in 5:11; and Elijah in 5:17–18). James employs distinctive Jewish terms: "twelve tribes in the Dispersion" (1:1), "Lord of hosts" (5:4), and "God is one" (2:19).

On the Greek side, the book was written originally in Greek. Old Testament quotations are from the Septuagint (the earliest Greek translation of the Old Testament done between 280 and 100 B.C.E.). James also uses sixty-three Greek words not used elsewhere in the New Testament, alliteration, rhyme, metaphors for the tongue involving horses and ships common in Greek literature, and the Greek rhetorical device of the hypothetical speaker.

James also gives evidence that its author was accustomed to public speaking. Besides oral devices such as the hypothetical speaker, alliteration, and rhyme, James repeats "my brothers and sisters" (actually, just "brothers" in Greek) twelve times to indicate the transition to a new subject. Some scholars even suggest that James was originally a sermon or is a careful reconstruction of pieces from several sermons. Thus, read the entire book aloud as you prepare to preach from it. Listen to it as a sermon to your life. This could be an important aid to its impact on you and on your listeners.

What preacher in the earliest church was able to incorporate elements of both Jewish and Greek thinking into a piece of Eastern wisdom writing? The most popular and apparent answer is James, the brother of Jesus (Mt. 13:55; Mk. 6:3; Acts 12:17). Other evidence points to a very early date of writing, making James perhaps the earliest of all New Testament books. Of Jesus' immediate family only his mother was a believer before Jesus' resurrection (Jn. 7:2–10). James was with the apostles at Pentecost (Acts 1:14) and was one to whom the resurrected Jesus appeared (1 Cor. 15:7). He became a major leader of the apostles very quickly (Gal. 1:19; 2:9; Acts 12:17; 15:12–21) but remained located in Jerusalem until his martyrdom in 61 C.E. (recorded by Josephus, a Jewish historian in the first Christian century). Some scholars think James wrote just before his death. Others even credit James's followers with assembling a representative collection of his teaching after James died. Evidence from the book itself points us in a far different direction. The book seems to assume believers are all Jewish, with not a whisper of Gentile converts or issues related to the Gentile controversies. This seems to place the letter before the formal decision of the Jerusalem council in 49 C.E., concerning what to do about Gentile converts. James appears to have chaired that council (Acts 15:13; compare 21:18; Gal. 1:19; 2:9, 12) and would surely have dealt with some of its issues had he written in the fifties as many scholars claim.

Our dating of this letter places it as the earliest connection of any New Testament writing to Jesus himself. The letter fascinates us with its frequent allusions to teachings of Jesus also found in the gospel of Matthew (written at the earliest around 70 C.E.). These allusions point especially to the Sermon on the Mount (Mt. 5–7). The clearest parallels are: James 1:12/Matthew 5:10–12; James 1:25/Matthew 7:21; James 5:2–3/Matthew 6:19–20; James 5:12/Matthew 5:33–37. James 1:19, 26; 3:1–12; 5:12 could stem from Jesus' teaching in Matthew 12:36, that at judgment people will have to account for "every careless word they have spoken."

We must ask, Where did James obtain his information about Jesus' teaching? Matthew's gospel could not have served as his source, for the letter was writen decades before Matthew's gospel. Not being a believer before the resurrection, James may never have heard any of Jesus' teaching firsthand. This means that quite soon after the resurrection, the early church must have collected and treasured a solid core of Jesus' teaching. As leader of the Jerusalem church, James quickly assimilated the Master's words into his own teaching. Yet James did not seem to think it necessary to tell readers that his teaching was grounded in the teaching of Jesus. Mention of "royal law" (2:8), suggesting Jesus' kingdom of God teaching, is the only hint of any kind. Were people so well versed in Jesus' teaching that it was as obvious to them, as it is to us, who have Matthew and can easily compare the two writings?

The fact that James intertwines his teaching and preaching with that of Jesus is instructive to all of us who preach and teach. Quoting scripture, the gospels, or even James is not so important as saturating ourselves with their insight, knowledge, and truth. Only then can we translate biblical teaching to others effortlessly through our lives and preaching as James did and does. Our lives become a window for others to see Christ's teaching growing and thriving in a real human specimen. For those of us who are preachers and teachers in Christ's church, untold numbers of people peer through the windows of our lives to get a peek at what a Christian is supposed to look and sound like. The added bonus is—if they hear us preach or teach each Sunday—they also get to hear us expound the truth of the gospel, hopefully in ways that inspire them to invigorate their lives by the power of the gospel as well.

Our hope is that this book will help you do this well, that it will help saturate your own life with the message of the book of James, so that you may expound it in ways that will enable your listeners to grow richly in their relationship with God.

To make this volume accessible to the widest possible audience, we have elected not to identify words by their Greek originals. Those who are using the Greek New Testament to prepare their sermons can readily observe what Greek word we are explaining. Those who are using the NRSV, the version used for this Chalice Press preaching series, will see the words as translated in the NRSV immediately in the text.

CHAPTER 1

Celebrating God in All Circumstances

JAMES 1:2–18

Exegesis

The letter of James opens with a campaign for seeing God's goodness all around us. This is not easy for people to do because life is not typically full of sweetness and light. Rather, it offers injustices, personal failures, and a never-ending quest for a real relationship with God. Yet, James is adamant that God's goodness is there to see, if we don the spiritual glasses that enable us to discern it.

In Trials (1:2–4)

In these verses, James sketches out a cycle that people must experience if the difficulties of life are to have meaning and purpose. Recognizing the truth of this cycle will help the believer celebrate God's goodness while living through it. The cycle comes in three stages.

The first stage is trial. By introducing the idea of trials with "whenever," James assumes that the Christian life–indeed, anyone's life–includes difficulties that must be worked through. By modifying trials with "of any kind," James shows that he has no particular kind of difficulty in mind. Many New Testament passages, such as 1 Peter, encourage persecuted Christians to remain faithful through trials and troubles. James is not so sharply focused. This letter, like much wisdom literature, looks at life more broadly. As human beings, Christians find that most of their troubles have more to do with being a neighbor, employee, husband, wife, or child, than with being a Christian per se. James brings up such specific situations throughout the letter (2:6; 3:2; 4:2, 11; 5:9, 13, 19). Belief in Christ does not give Christians an advantage over non-Christians in the area of enduring troubles. Christian faith does provide an advantage, James insists, in coping with and solving life's difficulties in a positive and successful way.

The question, then, is not whether or not Christians will encounter trials. Everyone who breathes faces trials. The central question is how we understand God's purposes for trials in our lives and how we cope with them in light of those purposes. Trials by definition have an undetermined outcome. That's why they are held! A secular trial may determine the post-position in an auto or horse race, or the guilt or innocence of a defendant.

To begin on the positive side, then, James assumes all believers have the potential to be successful in dealing with the trials that come their way. At the outset, without batting an eyelash, the letter can honestly admonish its readers to "consider it nothing but joy" when life hands them trials. Trials are opportunities rather than impossible obstacles.

Exactly what kind of opportunities these are becomes clearer in 1:3. Trials—all trials—are spiritual opportunities. All of them are a "testing of your faith." For most people "tests" are not viewed positively. Emotions of fear and anxiety plague us, making us think we will give wrong answers, or worse yet, fail an exam. Yet, tests are really neutral. A test for the quality of metals (where the Greek word used here originates), or soil, or beef, or anything else, measures a product against a quality control standard. Difficulties in life, James asserts, are opportunities for Christians to show the "metal" of their faith. Perfection is no more possible than for an ore to be 100 percent gold. We can, however, attain a certain quality level on a sliding scale of maturity. Trials can show us that our faith is real, that it can face difficult circumstances and come through them unscathed, still attached in trust and commitment to Christ.

This brings James to the second stage in the cycle of meaningful life. One must not only face trials, but James asserts that living through a period of trial or a specific difficulty successfully demands "endurance." Assuming Christians will live through their everyday difficulties, what does James assume could be lost amidst the tough days? The answer must be: "faith." James knows that sometimes even Christians go through tough times and fail to trust God. They may even lose trust in God altogether through such difficult circumstances. In such cases, James asserts that they didn't get past the first stage of the test. They neglected their faith in God, or worse yet, lost it, showing its unsatisfactory quality to begin with. The proper approach is to believe in God throughout the difficulty, drawing on as yet untapped potentials of faith in order to persevere, thus emerging with a higher quality of faith. Every athlete knows that the key to improvement is to face tougher competition. Only such competition can force muscles to strengthen and decision-making to improve. So it is, says James, with the growth of believers. Enduring life's trials brings new muscles to our faith.

The third stage in James's cycle of life's meaning is maturity. Facing a trial and enduring it with trust in God's purposes will lead to spiritual growth. Specifically, James speaks of being "mature and complete," or "perfect" and "entire" (*King James Version* [KJV]). The two words are synonyms and probably are intended to express one idea. Both can refer to a healthy body, but they do not in any way assume a sinless person. So, successfully completing the cycle of life's meaning in one instance does not make people "perfect" throughout their spiritual lives. It does, however, indicate that believers have reached a level of wholeness in at least one aspect of their spiritual lives and that they are one step closer to reaching their full potential of Christian maturity. This also makes them ready for a tougher trial next time, which, when successfully completed, will bring them to another level of maturity and one more step closer to full, spiritual growth.

In Prayer (1:5–8)

James's kinship to wisdom literature becomes incontestable in this section as it presents a recipe for coping successfully with life's trials. The recipe is simple: Ask for wisdom. A believer who cannot endure and grow in faith is "lacking" something. This something, James stresses, is readily available from God through prayer. Such availability encourages us and points us to God's goodness. The epistle calls this needed ingredient "wisdom," drawing on well-established wisdom teachings inside and outside the Jewish canon.

The Jewish perspective insists that wisdom is not about rational intelligence or being smart. It is about the skill to make good decisions in life. It is a personal characteristic that grows with age. Rarely do we call a young person "wise." We quite naturally, however, recognize wisdom in the experience of the elderly. Wisdom does not come simply through the aging process. It is not an innate trait waiting to burst forth at the appropriate moment. Rather, God is the storehouse of all wisdom. As creator and sustainer of the world, God holds the key to living successfully in it. Proverbs 2:6 says, "The LORD gives wisdom," a teaching given real life illustration in 1 Kings 3:28 and 4:29.

But how does a person gain such wisdom? If it does not evolve naturally from within, remaining instead in divine hands, how can I hope to attain it? James clearly picks up Jewish thought as he points us to wisdom's source. The first step toward God's wisdom for living is to know and honor God. Psalm 111:10 teaches us: "The fear of the LORD is the beginning of wisdom." Other passages reiterate this (Job 28:28; Prov. 1:7; Mic. 6:9). When fear of the Lord becomes a characteristic of life, you naturally turn to God in prayer to seek what is "lacking" in life.

Prayer brings you God's wisdom to make good choices in life's tough circumstances. Such prayer is not a one-time thing. One prayer does not bring wisdom for all of life's decisions. Believers who fear God pray repeatedly throughout life. In fact, each decision calls for prayer for wisdom. As believers receive what they recognize to be God's wise choice and act on it, their confidence in divine personal care for them increases. Such experiences of answered prayer prove God's availability. Through such experiences faith grows. This enables you to be more and more confident, not only of God's existence, but of God's personal love for you.

The prayer life of such a believer is stable and enriching. James could not imagine such a person second-guessing God or questioning divine wisdom and goodness. Only people whose Christianity is hollow question God's existence and goodness. Such people routinely function without God in their lives. Without faith, without perseverance, people find God unresponsive to their cries for assistance in times of trouble.

This faithless person without endurance goes to church but really isn't a believer. Today we might call such a person "two-faced" or a "hypocrite." James labels that person, "double-minded," or more literally in line with the Greek word for "double-souled," a word used only here in the New Testament. This "double-souled" person struggles with conflict over the authenticity of a personal relationship with God. She has not sold herself out in faith to her Creator and Savior.

James pictures this person as a "wave" on a choppy sea. At the wind's mercy this person of immature faith seemingly moves many directions at the same time. James does not use sea imagery to depict the faithful person, but implies such a description. A person with mature faith would be like a ship that sails steadily through the waves, employing the wind to aid its course. This is the exact opposite to the unsteady, windblown, last-minute, faith-in-a-foxhole type of person who cannot be assured of God's positive response for help.

James's teaching is consistent with Jesus' teaching on God's sure response to the prayers from people of faith (Mt. 7:7; 21:21; Mk. 11:22–24; Lk. 11:9). James added the emphasis that God responds "generously" and "ungrudgingly." Like parents who love their children deeply, God has no limits in supplying resources to aid believers through the tough times in life. God wants to respond to the prayers of the faithful whenever and wherever possible. James encourages believers not to hesitate for a second to ask for God's help. God has not placed a quota on how many requests one is allowed. God is not a genie in a bottle who grants just three wishes. Heavenly resources and love are limitless.

In Poverty and Wealth (1:9–11)

The social and economic situations of believers may vary, even reflecting extreme contrasts. However, their need to celebrate God and the divine goodness remains the same. So does their need to rely on God's help within their varying situations. The challenges life presents will be different, but every person—rich or poor—ultimately will face challenges to faith. You can always see these as opportunities for enhancing the spiritual growth cycle.

Later in the epistle James returns to the subject of the rich and the poor. He contrasts the way they are received in the public assembly of believers (2:2–7). He also chastises the rich for taking advantage of the poor (5:1–6). In those contexts James was not concerned about whether the poor or the rich were Christians. Both passages seem to assume that at least the rich were not. In this passage (1:9–11), however, the Greek grammar shows that both poor and rich at least consider themselves to be believers. The *New Revised Standard Version* (NRSV) quite properly translates the Greek word for "brother" as "believer," because this is the prevalent meaning of the word in the New Testament.

Some commentators insist that this epistle could not possibly consider any rich person to be a Christian. These scholars claim that the widespread famine in Palestine (Acts 11:28–29) and the Jewish community's ostracism of converts to Christianity would have left the entire Christian community poor. Paul's extensive labor among Gentile churches to provide relief funds for believers in Jerusalem (2 Cor. 8) also supports this view. Such historical reconstruction cannot override the clear meaning of the grammar and the point of James's illustration here. This passage does not work as an illustration of James's point unless both poor and rich are believers at least in name. James insists that both rich and poor will undergo the distinctive tests of life that fit their individual social standing. Besides, one must realize that James is writing to "the twelve tribes in the Dispersion," that is, scattered Jewish believers, not just the impoverished church at Jerusalem.

Believers at the bottom—and at the top—of the social spectrum will have trials. As they persevere in such trials, both rich and poor may see their faith flourish. Both are called upon to "boast" in the spiritual reversal of their human, social condition. The poor believer's "being raised up," or literally "his high position or status," assumes that this hypothetical believer has endured many trials, so common to the poor. Through such endurance the poor believer has successfully developed through the spiritual growth cycle to accumulate, as it were, a great wealth of faith. In other words, though the poor are usually considered "disadvantaged" because of their economic resources, in terms of spiritual opportunity to develop faith, they really have an advantage over the rich.

In contrast, the rich, normally considered advantaged in human life, are to celebrate "in being brought low." This may be translated more literally as "his humble" or "low" position or "his humiliation" or "his reversal of fortunes." The Greek text uses a word that comes from the same root word used originally to describe the poor. It seems impossible that a nonbelieving person of wealth could be expected to thank God for losing a fortune, whether to thieves or through the stock market. However, if the reversal description of the rich person as "low" or "humble" refers to spiritual condition—as "high" does in describing the poor person earlier—then such reversal is not only possible but necessary for a wealthy believer.

Whereas the spiritual trial for the poor is their lack of wealth, the spiritual trial for the rich is their ample resources. In everyday life wealth appears to makes people more important, but Christians with money must realize that their wealth does not mean anything in their value to God, who is concerned instead with their faith. In this area they are at a disadvantage to the poor. Their easy life easily makes God less of a necessity. To succeed as a believer, the wealthy, then, must recognize their economic advantage as a hindrance to their faith. Wealth becomes, in its inverse way, their trial. James presumes that most of the rich will fail in faith. Such people then become an example of the hollow-faithed person tossed by the wind of the world.

James turns to the farmer's field to illustrate his point. He compares the rich to a wild flower. For a brief moment in the lush days of spring, the blossom thrives, its colors brilliant. But it takes only a few days in the harsh summer's dry heat for the bloom's brilliance to fade, its petals drying up and falling off. So it is with the significance of the wealthy. They need to measure themselves with respect to God's eternity. Their wealth is but a blip on the divine screen's picture of humanity. They will die and face God in judgment like everyone else. They must stand before the divine Judge with no money, no lavish clothing. They must stand there with nothing but themselves and their faith, if they have any after the negative effects of a pampered life.

Will any wealthy make it to eternity? James would answer, "Not many," but he does not shut the door. Jesus concurs. In his parable of the rich fool (Lk. 12:13–21), the rich man hoards his wealth, building bigger barns to store his bumper crop. Jesus warns that the man would die "this very night" and face God's judgment with great material possessions but no faith in God. "So it is," Jesus concludes, "with those who store up treasure for themselves but are not rich toward God."

It is not surprising, then, that Jesus forced the rich young ruler to chose between following him as a disciple and keeping his possessions (Mt. 19:21). His ample possessions were not the spiritual asset he thought they were. Only two verses later, Jesus turned to his disciples to declare how hard it is for a rich man to enter the kingdom of heaven, more difficult than for "a camel to go through the eye of a needle" (Mt. 19:23–24). As James drives home, possessions are a threatening liability to faith and spiritual growth.

In Temptation (1:12–15)

People have a tendency to blame God for their troubles and their failures. Very much aware of this, James defends God's honor, indeed, the very nature of God. God allows for trials in life for our own good, but God is not the tempter. Rather, the Creator desires that people persevere and develop their faith through the various situations life offers.

James specifically links 1:12 back to 1:2–4 by repeating specific Greek words that James basically restricts to these two texts. "Test" occurs only in 1:13–14 in James, while *the noun form of the same word is translated as* "trials" and "temptation" in 1:2 and 1:12. Note NRSV's needless use of different English words here, when most translations use *trials* in both passages (RSV, NEB, NIV, TEV). To translate it "temptation" at 1:12 puts it into conflict with what 1:13 says, that God does not tempt anyone. "Testing" in 1:3 balances "stood the test" in 1:12. "Endurance" in 1:3–4 complements "endures" in 1:12. Note that these last two terms also appear in 5:11. Thus, similar to 1:2–4, James speaks of celebrating God's goodness in seeing people through difficulties to receive an eternal reward.

"Consider it nothing but joy" (v. 2) called on believers to celebrate God through trial. Verse 12 replaces this with *blessed,* meaning that "trials" or "temptation" represent an observable manifestation of God's goodness that ought to be recognized as such. Some translations, such as *Today's English Version* (TEV), *Jerusalem Bible* (JB), *New English Bible* (NEB), and *Living Bible* (LB) use *happy* instead of *blessed* for the Greek word here. However, *happy* is not really equivalent to *blessed*. Being happy is an emotional reaction to pleasing circumstances in life. James is talking about the opposite, about trials, tough times. One cannot be expected to be happy about facing difficulties. Being blessed involves God's perspective. God alone can make someone "blessed." God intends a positive outcome even in the difficulties we face.

This positive outcome is not only the perseverance itself but also a reward from God as the culmination of life, "the crown of life." Elsewhere in the New Testament, two different types of crowns are mentioned. Revelation (4:4, 10; 6:2; 12:1; 14:14) makes reference to royal crowns. However, 1 Corinthians 9:25 and 2 Timothy 2:5 picture successful believers receiving the kind of victory crowns made of bay or olive wreaths and given to winners of athletic contests in the Roman world (compare Phil. 4:1; 1 Thess. 2:19; 2 Tim. 4:8; 1 Pet. 5:4; Rev. 2:10; 3:11). This winner's crown seems to be in mind here, too. The believer wins the victory by overcoming the trials of life and thus receives the crown of life–God's ultimate eternal blessing. The qualification that makes victory possible is "love" for God. True success is really about building a love relationship of faith and trust in God through life's everyday struggles. Eternal life with God will result.

James 1:13–15 describes how the spiritual universe is organized. This passage seeks to set people straight on what God does and does not do. God is creator of all life but not of evil. Evil comes out of human rebellion, a rebellion made possible because God has given people free choice to obey or disobey their Creator. Adam and Eve are the prototypes. A tempter, an evil personality, lives in God's universe, but James carefully avoids mentioning the devil in this context so as not to give people another excuse for their sin. This tempter, named Satan elsewhere in the Bible (Job 1:6–12; Mt. 4:1–11; Lk. 4:1–13), enjoys the God-given liberty to draw people away from God. This gives people real moral and spiritual choices. As in Job, though, Satan's activity is only possible through God's permission. God has already defeated the claims of the devil against humanity on the cross through Christ's sacrifice.

James puts the onus of responsibility on each individual, and on the choices we sometimes make to do evil instead of following God's will. James does not portray either God or the devil as a scapegoat in this passage. God by definition and by nature has no association with evil, sin, or temptation. James implies that to blame the Deity for our sin is itself sin, a foolish and self-pitying affront to God.

The pathway to sin, James teaches, has stages. The temptation is followed by the inclination, on our part, to be influenced by the temptation, rather than turning our backs to it and choosing to please God instead. This middle stage provides us the opportunity to recognize temptation for what it is and retreat from it. But neither the temptation to sin nor the inclination to be influenced by this temptation is sin. Sin is the last stage, the conscious, premeditated choice and act.

Apparently building on his use of the word translated as *desire*, James personifies the temptation process as a prostitute's seduction. Within this, two wildlife metaphors are employed. The word *lured*, only used here in the New Testament, relates to dragging away fish caught in a fishing net (see *New International Version* [NIV] translation). The word *enticed* relates to leaving bait in a hunting trap to capture wild animals. Such are the wiles of prostitutes and the cunning of our own desire as it works to ensnare us in sin. In a world without contraceptives, conception and childbirth by prostitutes was much more of a possibility than it is today. Thus, James pictures "birth" as the evidence of sin. A "fully-grown" illegitimate child becomes the equivalent of a sin or a life of sin that reaps God's condemning judgment, "death." The one who receives this judgment cannot blame God. God has not caused the temptation. God has been willing and ready to give wisdom that leads out of temptation. God has been aware of our trials and is able to show the way of faith through those trials. "Death" is the judgment of the divine court only when our faith does not mature and our love for God does not endure. Then we answer sin's call and bring death on ourselves.

In Life's Gifts (1:16–18)

James makes it unmistakably clear that God in no way deserves the blame for human sin. James moves on to identify God with every good thing that happens to people in their lives. This is the capstone to this section. God is to be celebrated in the tough times, the primary focus of James's teaching up to this point. But life has good times, too—wonderful moments in which we feel like someone indeed cares and is watching over us. These times, James emphasizes, come from God, who does love us.

In a sense, the NRSV's attachment of 1:16 to 1:12–15 is understandable. The warning about deception is most likely about believing that God is in the business of tempting people to sin. Yet the Greek grammar shows that other translations—such as the *Revised Standard Version* (RSV)—are right to recognize that 1:16 is a lead-in to what follows. This implies without overt statement that James's warning about being deceived applies to people who think the good things they experience are the result of their own achievements. In other words, we tend to blame God for the bad and take credit for the good ourselves, when it should actually be reversed.

James locates all the good that happens to people in God's loving character by describing God as the "Father of lights."

This is a curious phrase connecting God first with the creation of light from darkness, but more specifically the creation of the sun and the stars. In Jewish thinking, light symbolizes purity, goodness, and truth, while darkness represents deception, evil, and falsehood. The constancy of God's pure character is emphasized when it is said that "there is no variation or shadow due to change." As the sun moves through the sky during the day, shadows come and go, changing constantly. God's character is not like that. With God it is always shadowless high noon. The divine character is perfectly pure. This explains, then, why God only brings things into our lives for our good, whether they are trials or gifts or things in-between.

In 1:18 James makes a brilliant move to describe God's greatest gift to humanity in language that still connects to creation. The language parallels the creation of Adam and Eve, to whom God gave dominion over the rest of creation (Gen. 1:28). However, the meaning must also refer to the spiritual rebirth of people into Christianity:

1. What is said is introduced as the culmination of God's purposes.
2. The word *us* implies believers.
3. The inducement for birth is described not just as the word but as the "word of truth," a term for the gospel (Col. 1:5; Eph. 1:13; and 2 Tim. 2:15).
4. The language of birth or rebirth commonly refers to Christian conversion in the New Testament (Jn. 3:3; 1 Pet. 1:3).
5. "First fruits" can refer to Christians in relationship to unconverted humanity (Rom. 16:5 and 1 Cor. 15:23).

The language of birth in 1:18 intends to contrast dramatically with its use in 1:15, where sin gives birth ultimately to death. In a sense James implies two types of new birth. New birth through sin leads to God's judgment. New birth through acceptance of the word of truth brings resurrection to new life and ultimately eternal life with God.

SERMON ONE ▰▰▰▰▰▰▰▰▰▰▰▰▰▰▰

Smiling through the Tears

(James 1:2–4)

Long before Elton John's and Tim Rice's song *The Circle of Life* became popular as the theme of the Disney classic *The Lion King*, James introduced a similar concept to the first-century church. Life is a cycle, and those who recognize it will be able to cope with its various phases.

Smile–You Will Have Tough Times!

The moments I dreaded most in school were those class periods when the teacher started the lesson with these words, "Close your book, and take out a blank sheet of paper." The ominous, unannounced pop quiz was a killer. My palms immediately began to sweat, and my mind started racing. "Have I read enough? Do I have a grasp on what we've been studying in this class? How much will this affect my final grade?" It is amazing how many issues one's mind can focus on while digging out a clean sheet of paper. In retrospect, what made the pop quiz so fearsome was the element of surprise. Just when you thought you had your teacher figured out, she would shatter your confidence by giving a surprise test.

Life is filled with pop quizzes. These are the tough times James calls trials. The struggles and difficulties of daily living are not selective, and no one is exempt from their hardships. These "tests" come unannounced and immediately create a sense of dread. "Can I handle this situation? Do I have enough confidence to survive? Why did God allow this to happen to me? How much will this affect my final grade?"

James wrote to a first-century church composed predominately of Jewish Christians. These disciples, who were scattered among the many Mediterranean communities, knew what tough times were all about. Jewish kinsmen had rejected and persecuted them. The Gentile elite abused and exploited them. They understood what it meant to endure unannounced trials and tests on a daily basis.

When James penned his letter to these struggling believers, he did not begin with a word of sympathy for their circumstances. Nor did he incite a spirit of revolution to fight back. Rather, he opened with these remarkable words, "Consider it pure joy, my brothers, whenever you face trials of many kinds!" (Jas. 1:2, NIV). Two incredible thoughts leap out of James's initial imperative. The first is the inevitability of tough times. James did not write, "If you face trial..." He wrote, "Whenever you face trials..." In John 16:33, Jesus says, "In the world you face persecution." Job 5:7 says, "But human beings are born to trouble / just as sparks fly upward." You cannot get around this truth: Tough times will come! No exemption process is available. No 4-F status will be granted against being drafted into various trials; no note from your doctor will keep you from participating in tough times.

Tough times are no respecter of age. They accompany our lives from our earliest memories until we draw our last breaths. When Rebekah, our youngest daughter, was seven years old, she had one of those tough days, at least from the perspective of a seven year old. That evening I found an "anonymous" note on my desk. I have treasured this note through the years, and we have laughed about it many times. It reads as follows (her spelling intact):

> Dad, I'm not sorry. It's been the worst day of my whole life. I got in a fight with Sarah. I got a minus one on my spelling test. And you made me punch my cheek and it hert. And mom got mad at me. I have to take the spelling test all over again. And I lost my nickel for snack money. The food wasn't good at lunch today. It has been a teribble, horrible no good very bad day. from, ???

It didn't require the skills of a Sherlock Holmes to deduce the identity of the author. Rebekah had experienced, for her, the worst day imaginable. At some earlier date, Elsie and I had read her Judith Viorst's children's book *Alexander and the Terrible, Horrible, No Good, Very Bad Day.*[1] Rebekah was identifying with his troubles. Have you ever had a terrible, horrible, no good, very bad day? Of course you have—that's life. The tough times do not ease up as we age. We go from lost nickels to lost jobs, from spelling tests to medical tests, and from childhood squabbles to battling life-threatening diseases. James was right! When it comes to tough times, it is never a question of "if," but rather "whenever."

James's second thought is even more incredible than the first. He reminds us that going through tough times ought to be considered pure joy. How can that be? Joy is an attitude based on a relationship with God. A Christian who views the tough times through the lens of joy will view trials as opportunities and not obstacles. When that occurs, the cycle continues.

Smile—You Can Persevere!

God never wastes a trial. My grandparents' generation came through a period of American history when very little was considered disposable. They raised their families during the Great Depression of the 1930s, and nothing was wasted that might be used on another occasion. Something as insignificant as a rusty, bent nail was straightened and put into a coffee can with similarly redeemed nails to be used on the next project. Farmers who butchered their own meat wasted nothing. It was often said that every part of the pig was used except the squeal.

While we might not take such heroic measures to save a rusty nail today, most of us do not want to be wasteful. What is true of things can be even truer of one's time and experiences. James reminded his readers that God never wastes a tough time. Billy Graham put it this way, "Mountaintops are for views and inspiration, but fruit is grown in the valleys."[2] Tough times are the valleys where the fruit of our faith is tested. Those pop quizzes in school were neither good nor bad; they were neutral. They only provided an opportunity for students to demonstrate what knowledge they possessed. In similar fashion, the tough times of life provide Christians with the opportunity to demonstrate whether or not we truly believe what we profess. Anyone can have strong faith when all is well, but what happens when the tide turns and adversity strikes like a tidal wave? Will our anchor of faith be strong enough to hold? Here's the ironic twist: No one enjoys the trials of life, but without them we would never know the true strength of our faith.

As the cycle of faith continues, it should produce in the believer a spirit of perseverance or endurance. This noun *perseverance* literally means, "a remaining under."[3] Perseverance is more than just patience. It is the ability to take a tough situation and turn it into a great victory. Think of a soldier standing ground and achieving a victory on the battlefield against all the odds. Through life's trials the Christian develops a steadfast attitude that will not retreat nor give up when the tough times come.

At just 5-foot-10 and 202 pounds, Walter Payton was not a particularly big running back in the National Football League, but he set one of sport's greatest records at the time: the all-time rushing record of 16,726 yards. That means during his twelve-year career, Payton carried the football over nine miles! That's impressive enough. Remember, too, that during those nine miles someone bigger than Payton knocked him to the ground, on average, every 4.4 yards. That makes his record demand even more respect. All through those twelve seasons, he kept getting up, and getting up, and getting up again. Great victories await those with great endurance.[4]

The cycle continues.

Smile–You Will Grow Up!

The tough times lead to endurance, and endurance leads to maturity–potentially! It's not a given, but the opportunity is there. Growing old is inevitable; maturity, however, remains optional. An anonymous sage penned these words: "You are only young once, but you can stay immature indefinitely." James's letter is about growing up in Christ, and he wastes no time in confronting the reader with this challenge. How does one measure the maturing process? Maturity comes when one discovers that life's problems and crises are not the occasion for tragedy, but the opportunity for triumph!

Little children love the word *why*. In the early years, they can become downright obnoxious with their constant desire to know "why." If we were honest with ourselves, we adults would admit that we love the word *why* too; we just don't ask it as often as a three year old. Maybe we should. When you and I understand the "why" of our tough times, the tough times become more tolerable. I considered those pop quizzes in school to be a lot of things, but "pure joy" was not one of them! But whenever I learned that I had scored an A, I experienced a sense of great satisfaction. I found myself saying, "That wasn't so bad after all!"

While no trial or difficulty is a picnic, what is learned through the process is often invaluable. And that knowledge—as painful as it may be to learn—will bring a sense of growing joy. That's why William Baker writes (in the exegesis section above), "The question, then, is not whether or not Christians will encounter trials. Everyone who breathes faces trials. The central question is how we understand God's purposes for trials in our lives and how we cope with them in light of those purposes." A Christian who pursues God's purpose in the trials of life is well on the way to finding mature joy, even in the test.

Author Jill Briscoe was scheduled to speak at a ladies' conference in Australia. Her daughter was going along for a vacation. The day before they left, Jill hurt her back. By the time they arrived in Australia, she had to be carried off the airplane. Together, she and her daughter worked to share the seminar. That painful experience opened up a whole new ministry for mother and daughter. Jill wrote afterwards, "I have often revisited the lessons we learned on our trip. Above all, I've tried not to 'waste' the pain that God allows in my life—to let the pain drive me to Him, not away from Him—and to be thankful in all circumstances."[5]

God never wastes a tough time! Such is the power and promise of God's circle of life.

SERMON TWO

Surviving through Temptation

(James 1:13-18)

Temptation is as common and inclusive as tough times. No one is exempt—young or old, rich or poor—all are tempted to sin. The difference between temptation and tough times is simple. Tough times are most often beyond our control, but resisting temptation is not. Struggling with tough times will not necessarily lead to temptation, but yielding to temptation will inevitably lead to tough times.

To be tempted is to be enticed, coerced, confronted with pleasure. It is to be drawn in by false promises. Temptation comes to the child who looks longingly into the toy store window and is intent on fulfilling his or her heart's desire with everything that is there.

Tempted to Blame God

God is never so conspicuously present as when we are looking for a place to lay the blame. I like the story of the preacher whose New Year's resolution was to cut back on the donuts he loved so much. On his first day back to work, he had to pass the donut shop on his drive to the church office. The closer he got, the stronger the temptation became to stop for fresh donuts. His only recourse was to pray intensely. When he arrived at the office, he walked in carrying a box of fresh donuts. His secretary looked surprised and asked about his resolution. "It's God's will—I prayed, 'Lord, if you want me to have donuts make a parking space available right in front of the shop.' Sure enough, on the ninth time around the block, there was the parking space."

This temptation "blame game" is nothing new. Our ancient ancestors—Adam and Eve—tried to find a scapegoat for their sin and disobedience in the Garden. (Since there were only two of them in Eden, that argument must have become real personal!) Notice Adam's expertise at placing blame: "The woman whom you gave to be with me, she gave me fruit from the tree, and I ate" (Gen. 3:12). In a handful of words he attacked both Eve and God, but mostly God. Adam's descendants have all inherited this same tendency: when we sin, it must be God's fault. One might erroneously conclude, "If I pray before I sin, it might turn out to be God's will." James wrote to dispute such faulty logic.

James makes it clear that "God cannot be tempted" or be a tempter. The Greek word here (*apeirastos*) is a strong term, used here for the only time in the New Testament. It means that

God is incapable of being tempted. In other words, God is "untemptable."[6]

God has no acquaintance with evil or contact with wickedness. Evil and God are at opposite ends of the spectrum. Since God has no connection with evil, there is no possible way for God to lead someone to do an evil deed. James further deepens the contrast in verse 17, describing God as the "Father of lights, with whom there is no variation or shadow due to change." Once again James's logic is irrefutable: Evil is represented by darkness. God is consistent light (no shadows). That means God can only be the source of good. God is incapable of doing anything but good! The whole point of this logical argument is to convince the reader that when a person sins, that person must not—no, cannot—point the finger of blame at God.

Being Tempted to Excuse Ourselves

Have you ever known someone who is never wrong, no matter how blatant and obvious an error the person has made? Such obnoxious behavior often leads one to angrily claim innocence at the cost of all logic and evidence. Unfortunately, we are all at times guilty of that uncomely attitude. Each of us has moments when we simply refuse to listen or acknowledge the error of our ways. I made the mistake! I made the bad decision! My bad! I made a poor choice! I sinned! Hard to say, isn't it?

What we dislike in others we are most likely to excuse in ourselves. When we excuse ourselves, we also deceive ourselves. The more judgmental we are of others, the less likely we are to take an honest look at ourselves. Placing the blame on others while excusing ourselves seems to come naturally for most people. Comedian Flip Wilson popularized this whole concept in the 60s and 70s with his famous character Geraldine and her often-used quote, "The devil made me do it." We would like to believe Geraldine rather than God. Sin is not my fault; it's the devil's fault. By the way, that excuse wasn't original with Flip Wilson. Eve has the original copyright on this popular concept: "The serpent tricked me, and I ate" (Gen. 3:13). Take a good look in the mirror. Don't forget what you see. When you sin, you have no one to blame but the one staring back at you.

When we are persuaded to excuse our guilt, we need to read James 1:14 again and again, "But one is tempted by one's own desire, being lured and enticed by it."

This often-quoted piece of poetry bears repeating:

Two natures beat within my breast,
One is foul, the other blest.
The one I love, the one I hate,
But the one I feed will dominate.[7]

Why do we struggle with temptation so much? Because it looks so good and feels so right! Have you ever been tempted to have a root canal? Of course not! Dental work, in general, is not a pleasant, enjoyable experience. Sin would never be an issue if every violation were the equivalent of having an amputation. Notice the word *enticed* in verse 14. Think of the word *enticed* as baiting a hook. Everyone who fishes understands the purpose of a baited hook. The bait entices; the hook ensnares. When you watch someone reel in a five-pound bass, do you ever stop to think how many baited hooks that experienced bass ignored until the one drifted by that could no longer be ignored? After all, a five-pound bass doesn't grow to that size overnight. For years that fish has watched the baited hooks bob in the water without giving them a second glance. Today, a shiny lure caught his eye. He followed it through the water: nibble, nibble, chomp, ZING! The reel begins her high-pitched sorrowful wail that announces a death sentence for the old fish.

We can't ever let our guards down. We never know when we are about to bite a baited hook. And there are a lot of baited hooks out there. Leann Birch, a developmental psychologist at Penn State University, ran an experiment in which she took a large group of kids and fed them a big lunch. Then she turned them loose in a room with lots of junk food.

"What we see is that some kids eat almost nothing," she said. "But other kids really chow down, and one of the things that predicts how much they eat is the extent to which parents have restricted their access to high-fat, high-sugar food in the past: the more the kids have been restricted, the more they eat." Birch's study concluded that the children assumed the junk food would taste good primarily because they had been told that junk food was bad for them![8]

Part of our problem is our human nature that responds with abandon when we are told "no." We not only break the law because it is trying to control our sinful natures, but we convince ourselves that it's really a lot of fun, that it really tastes good—even when our relationship with God is at risk.

James 1:15 reminds us, "then, when that desire has conceived, it gives birth to sin, and that sin, when it is fully grown, gives birth to death."

No area of life is exempt from temptation, and the end result is always death. When the teacher gives a test, what's the temptation? We are tempted to cheat. If you lose your job, what is the temptation? You are tempted to take revenge. How many times have we witnessed a bitter employee returning to the place of former employment and unloading an automatic weapon on innocent coworkers? Marriage troubles lead to the temptation to have an affair or snatch the kids. Financial troubles lead to the temptation to embezzle or borrow with no intention of repaying. Crises with children often tempt parents to ignore the problem in the hope that the problems will simply go away. The list is endless. We are tempted emotionally, intellectually, physically, financially, socially, and spiritually. Trust me—Satan knows where to drop the baited hook!

King David's leadership was seriously undermined by his one-night fling with Bathsheba (2 Sam. 11). He paid an incredible price in his reign as king and in his family when he compromised his moral integrity for one fleeting moment. In his book *Temptation*, Dietrich Bonhoeffer wisely strikes at the heart of the problem:

> In our members there is a slumbering inclination toward desire, which is both sudden and fierce. With irresistible power, desire seizes mastery of the flesh. All at once a secret, smoldering fire is kindled...It makes no

difference whether it is a sexual desire, or ambition, or vanity, or desire for revenge, or love of fame and power, or greed for money...At this moment God is quite unreal to us. He loses all reality, and only desire for the creature is real...Satan does not here fill us with hatred of God, but with forgetfulness of God.[9]

I once heard Bob Russell (minister, Southeast Christian Church, Louisville) say in a sermon, "The pain of the harvest always exceeds the pleasure of the sowing."

We are up against an awesome enemy who wants to destroy our relationship with the Lord more than anything else in this universe: "For our struggle is not against enemies of blood and flesh, but against the rulers, against the authorities, against the cosmic powers of this present darkness, against the spiritual forces of evil in the heavenly places" (Eph. 6:12).

Forces that you and I cannot see are at war with the purposes of God, and we are the spoils of the battle. That's why we must resist. Someone put it this way. "Never give the devil a ride. The devil will always want to drive." When you travel with Satan, Satan plans the trip and picks the destination. And I'm telling you, you don't want to end up at that destination. So resist!

I like the story of the boxer who went into the ring against a bigger, stronger opponent and got whipped in the first round. He walked back to the stool at the sound of the bell, and his trainer patted him on the back and said, "You go back in there and get him this time. He hasn't laid a glove on you." The second round was worse than the first, and he shuffled back to the stool, head hanging low at the sound of the bell. The trainer patted him on the back again and said, "You go back in there and get him this time. He hasn't laid a glove on you." The boxer barely survived the third round, being saved from the count of ten only by the bell. He crawled back over to his stool in the corner and plopped down. The trainer patted him on the back and said, "You go back in there and get him this time. He hasn't laid a glove on you." The boxer looked at his trainer through his puffy eyes and said, "All right, I'll get him this time, but you keep your eyes on that referee, because somebody is beating me to a pulp." That is how Satan works in our lives, attacking from our blind side. So be prepared—don't take it on the chin. Resist!

Here is the bottom line—trust Jesus. If you do not like your relationship with Jesus, the devil will always take you back. Satan has a very generous return policy—anytime you want to bring your soul back, you'll be given full credit, without a receipt.

The contrast is that you can come near to God. I have told my daughters on numerous occasions, "If you need me, just call! If you've got a problem, if you get stranded with car trouble, whatever the issue, just call." Any loving father would do the same. God is like that. Just call! Your Parent in heaven will be there for you! God has not left us defenseless in this battle. Knowing we would blame the Creator and excuse ourselves, God promised us: "No test or temptation that comes your way is beyond the course of what others have had to face. All you need to remember is that God will never let you down; never let you be pushed past your limit; always be there to help you come through it" (1 Cor. 10:13, *The Message*). NRSV ends with, "he will also provide the way out."

Finally, let me suggest three simple escape lessons to help you survive temptation:

1. Avoid temptation as much as you can. In an episode of the old *Hee Haw* show, a patient complained to Doc Campbell, "Doc, I broke my arm in two places." Doc replied, "Well then, stay out of those places." If you know something or somewhere that offers strong temptation for you, stay away.

2. When you are tempted, run as fast as you can. Get away, escape, wriggle out of the coat. No possession or momentary enjoyment is worth the price of your integrity and relationship with God. If you can't run, read! The word of God is filled with encouraging passages to help one resist. It is easier to resist when you are reading the Bible. Don't let your anger lead you to make things worse! Listen more, respond less, and don't lose your temper.

3. If you fall, get up as soon as you can. Don't stay down when you yield to temptation as if there were no redemption. Don't give up; get up! God extends grace to those who ask for it with repentant hearts. The Lord wants you to experience a victorious life through Jesus Christ. You can learn to survive temptation! You can even learn to resist temptation! Start doing so today.

CHAPTER 2

Harnessing Our Life for God
JAMES 1:19–27

Exegesis

James ended the previous section by mentioning believers' new birth into Christianity and their role as "first fruits" (1:18). This leads James to motivate believers to grow in their faith so they can live it out in a way that rises above the behavior of others around them. Only in this way can believers call attention to the superiority of Christianity over other competing religions and philosophies.

James focuses on the spiritual discipline of control, a reverberating theme in wisdom literature both inside and outside the Bible. James teaches that control of anger, of behavior, and of speech are paramount for a Christian's life. Only such control lets believers witness to their "[re]birth by the word of truth." With poetic flair, James weaves these three concerns together into a simple proverb that both captures the essence of the issue and provides an outline for further expanding thoughts on each aspect.

New Life Guidelines Encapsulated in a Proverb (1:19)

Wisdom literature–Jewish and Greek, canonical and noncanonical–concerns itself with each of the three parts of this proverb. But no proverb in any of these sources connects the human behaviors of anger, speech, and listening. This brilliant proverb contains very practical wisdom for general humanity as well as for believers. People in James's day or ours can control regretful and embarrassing fits of anger by paying closer attention to other people when they speak, and by disciplining their own speech. Indeed, listening usually leads to controlled speech. This, in turn, prevents many kinds of angry speech we would later regret.

The book of Proverbs lauds the virtues of listening (5:1–2; 6:20–22; 15:31; 19:20; 22:17–18), controlled speech (10:8, 10, 19; 13:3; 18:2), and controlled anger (10:10; 12:16; 14:17, 19; 15:18; 16:32; 17:27; 20:3, 11; 29:11, 20, 22) as separate concerns. Indeed, we should discipline ourselves so that we improve in each of the three areas separately. We should listen to teachers, parents, spouses, bosses, and friends. We should be wise about when to speak and what to say to such people. We should prevent our lips from spouting angry words for which apologies will later be required. Each of these are worthy growth areas for everyone, believer and nonbeliever. James was not content simply to look at each area separately. He insists that the three areas impact one another, so he forms the three-part proverb of verse 19 and then unpacks the proverb's teaching on each of these three disciplines: 1:20–21 slow to anger; 1:22–25 quick to listen; and 1:26–27 slow to speak. In so doing, James offers much greater spiritual depth in each of these areas than what we expected on first reading the proverb.

"Quick to listen" becomes an admonition to hear God's word of truth and translate it obediently into compatible behavior. Listening to God, of course, is a prominent Old Testament theme (Deut. 5:1; 6:3–4; 9:1; 20:3; 1 Sam. 12:14–15; Jer. 7:24–27; Amos 3:1; 4:1; 5:1; Micah 1:2; 3:1, 7; Zech. 7:11–12; Mal. 2:2). "Slow to speak" becomes a barometer of Christianity's effectiveness in a believer's life. "Slow to anger" becomes the motivation for cleaning out all unrighteousness from one's life to allow the word of truth to flourish.

The three parts of the proverb do more than introduce the concerns of this section of James. They introduce the themes that will be developed in even more detail in the ensuing chapters: James 2–correctly hearing the word; James 3–the difficulty of controlling the tongue; James 4–the damaging effect of angry speech.

Control Anger by Purifying Oneself (1:20–21)

Assuming the proverb as a whole is self-explanatory, James made no effort to expand on the proverb itself. Rather, James isolated the third part and developed further concerns based on it. Display of anger in people, including believers, James observed, is but the outward sign of inward, spiritual problems. A remedy that goes much deeper than simply listening or controlling speech is available. This remedy involves honestly facing unrighteous attitudes and welcoming the influence of the word of truth personally.

Anger in itself is not sin. It is a human emotion God has given people as an outlet to deal with their frustrations in life as well as to help identify problems they need to deal with. The trouble comes with how people cope with their anger. Is its energy siphoned off to generate positive attention to resolve a problem? Or does it explode into saying and doing sinful and hurtful things? In the latter case anger becomes a problem and must be controlled. To fail to do so puts one in the unsatisfactory position of living in a manner utterly opposed to the way God desires for us to live. James assumes his readers desire to please God by living according to divine standards. Uncontrolled displays of anger do not fit into this category.

God's own righteous character does not allow for fits of rage, temper tantrums, or angrily zapping people. God does not think or act unkindly or unlovingly about anyone, ever. Nor should those who desire to emulate God's character.

James did not deny that God condemns people in acts of judgment. However, exacting punishment for sin is not an act of anger any more than a judge's sentencing of a criminal should be.

James wants us to see that an uncontrolled display of anger is the unrighteous behavior people most easily identify among all the unrighteous acts humans perform. Along with it, a host of actions and attitudes need to be expunged from people's lives. James simply grouped these together as "all sordidness and rank growth of wickedness" or "all moral filth and the evil" (NIV). The Greek word translated as "sordidness" appears only here in the New Testament. Related words are used in James 2:2; 1 Peter 3:21; Revelation 22:11. The word group literally refers to something that is disgustingly smelly or dirty. James described morally sinful activity with which people sometimes degrade themselves.

"Rank growth of wickedness" is the NRSV's attempt to convey two Greek words, literally translated "abundance of evil." Think of evil as overgrown weeds encroaching upon what is supposed to be a cultivated garden. James challenges readers to take on the task of cutting back the weeds of wickedness in their lives so that righteousness can flower and grow.

Fitting in with the garden imagery, James reminds readers that if they are believers, the seed of righteousness has already been planted in the fertile ground of their lives. They simply need to provide it room to spread so that righteousness can dominate their lives instead of unrighteousness. This seed, specifically described as "the implanted word," abbreviates "the word of truth" by which God "gave us birth" (1:18). This refers to the truth found in the gospel, the only word that has "the power to save your souls."

The new birth means all believers have the word of truth already implanted in them, just as every baby is born with hunger to eat, a mind to reason, and the desire to know God. All these require nurture in the growing infant. So does the gospel in the born-again person. James encourages us to "welcome" the special word as guest in the homes of our lives, to not hide it in the closet or the basement anymore. We need the gospel's growing influence if we are to live the kind of righteous lives God desires. Paul writes something very similar about "the word of God" in 1 Thessalonians 2:13.

What James writes here may be equated with what New Testament writers more commonly refer to as the role of Holy Spirit, who is given to people upon their conversion and baptism (Rom. 6). The Holy Spirit offers believers the power to overcome their continuing temptation to sin even after they have become Christians (Rom. 8).

Control Behavior by Hearing God's Word (1:22–25)

In verse 20 James dealt with the last member of verse 19's three-part proverb, namely anger. Verse 21 with its reference to "the implanted word" began to shift attention to the first member of the proverb. "Listen" now occupies center stage in verses 22–25. Listening is deepened beyond the physical act of hearing. James expands on the word and its power when activated to transform the lives of believers in ways pleasing to God.

Being "doers of the word" should come naturally to believers, in whom the word is implanted. Believers should operate life by one rule. Hear God's word with conviction and obedience. That means, let God's word control all our behavior.

As anyone who has children or teaches children knows a huge difference separates hearing and listening. Children can hear instructions, but they have not listened if they do not know how to do the assigned task. Listening presumes understanding so that the task can be performed well. One can hear words but not understand or care to understand.

James applied this distinction to Christian behavior. He calls on Christians not to remain self-deceived, thinking their relationship with God is in good order when, in fact, they do not control their behavior according to "the implanted word." This disjunction between hearing and listening is serious and requires radical change in lifestyle for anyone to truly be a Christian.

James insists that the word must be so integrated into believers' lives they will recognize when and how that word applies to each situation in life. Not to understand it or recognize its life applications is inconceivable and can be explained only as people not caring to know or apply the divine word. The mirror illustration is all the more powerful when you realize that the NRSV's "look at themselves," (v. 23) is more emphatic in Greek, reading literally, "the one who contemplates the face of his birth." The irony of not recognizing oneself is heightened by the fact that this is one's very own face that you have studied in the mirror for a lifetime. Thus, a Christian who does not know how to do the word is not who he or she claims to be. Such a person has a split personality, appearing to be a believer but not behaving as a believer behaves. This is not at all acceptable. The believer must be a doer.

James sets up a contrast between those who hear and do and those who hear and don't do. The first group (v. 25) "look

into the perfect law," see what they are to do, and immediately
do it. They integrate the word into their lives and understand
when and where it applies. In this case James uses a different
word for "look," emphasizing a brief look or a fleeting glance.
For hearers who do the word, just a quick glance at the word
results in appropriate behavior. This is far superior even to
prolonged study of the word without positive action.

James conscientiously switched from "word" in 1:22–24 to
"law" in 1:25 because he is talking about internal and external
aspects of the same thing: "Word" fits better God's internal
influence on the behavior of believers; "law" fits better external
principles that believers actually put into practice. This "law"
is described as both "perfect" and related to "liberty." The latter
term makes us take notice. The reference is not to the Old
Testament as a whole or to its laws in particular. To understand
James's meaning, we must take our cue from the reference to
"law of liberty" and other contexts that James anticipates.

In 2:8–13 "the law of liberty" will also be called "the royal
law": "You shall love your neighbor as yourself." This appears
in Leviticus 19:18, but "royal" connects the reference here to
him who came preaching the kingdom of God (Mk. 1:15) and
was crucified as "King of the Jews" (Mt. 27:37). Jesus is the one
who made this one law the backbone of all moral teaching.

Jesus said the "law" of neighbor love encapsulates the whole
law (Mt. 22:39; Mk. 12:31–33; Lk. 11:25–27) and so is really
no law at all in the proper sense. It is a principle of behavior
that frees one from being shackled to unwieldy laws in situations
that call for personal decisions. Thus, calling this "law" of
neighbor love a law of "liberty" is completely appropriate and
in line with James's desire for believers to enact the word in
their personal lives. Jeremiah 31:33 promised that one day the
law would be written on the hearts of God's people, a promise
fulfilled in Jesus' love ethic for the new kingdom. James expects
his readers to have this word implanted on their hearts to such
a degree that they could understand it, apply it, and obey it.

Being doers of the word is not a haphazard, hit or miss, on
again, off again mode of behavior. James insists we must
"persevere." Looking to the law of liberty as the guide to
controlling behavior is to be an integral pattern characterizing

believers' lives. This is not the same Greek word that the NRSV translates as "endurance" in 1:2–4 and 1:12. The Greek word for "persevere" here is a synonym that emphasizes continuing to be grounded or standing fast in something, no matter the changing conditions.

Finally, James announces that blessing from God will come to those who live by this guide. As with those who resist temptation in 1:12, God will approve as righteous those persons whose actions stem from a conscientious application of the law of liberty. They will experience God's goodness as they are obedient and loving to their neighbors.

Control Speech to Show the Truthfulness of Christianity (1:26–27)

James concludes the section by focusing on the middle part of the three-part proverb. Christian ethical discussions easily ignore human communication. James raises communication to a central place in Christian behavior. Such communication often demonstrates whether God's word of neighbor love controls believers' lives. We relate to others much more in words than in action. We also deceive and demean more than we murder and steal. As much as helping the poor, the talk of believers between themselves and with others provides an ideal opportunity to demonstrate that Christ truly controls our lives. People inside and outside the Christian faith will quickly notice if our talk reflects the Christian walk. Believers can measure their own personal spiritual development by focusing on their conversations and their dealings with the poor.

Once again James brings up the issue of self-deception. Not only are believers who hear but do not do self-deceived about their saving relationship with God (1:22), so are those who fail to "bridle their tongues." The image here is humorous as we try to picture a horse bridle being placed over a person's head to control the individual's tongue. The teaching may seem awfully harsh. Yet, Jesus was no less harsh when he taught: "I tell you, on the day of judgment you will have to give an account for every careless word you utter; for by your words you will be justified, and by your words you will be condemned" (Mt. 12:36–37).

A person's talk reveals the person's true character and identity: People who speak in vulgarities, people who lie, people who ridicule, and people who spread rumors and gossip readily demonstrate their general disregard for people as well as the lack of God's influence in their lives. People who think about how their speech will effect others, who use their words to build people up, and people who strive for honest communication are freely living by the law of neighbor love, and show that God is working through them.

James teaches that Christianity is unique in the way it can make people better people. One observes this unique "better" quality in the speech habits of God's people. James goes further to state that you can fairly assess a religion by the speech habits of its adherents.

When James wrote, only Judaism and Christianity believed in one God. All other peoples and nations worshiped aspects of nature or had developed philosophies of multiple gods to account for the world as they observed it. Nevertheless, religions even today—no matter how offbeat—have expectations of their followers. What James wanted to know is: Does a religion make an adherent a better person in her or his personal relationships, as measured by speech habits, and in community relationships, as observed in outreach to the poor and neglected?

If a religion is just a system of ideas with no impact on the everyday lives of its followers, then it has no value at all. Christianity in no way is the only religion to be able to influence people to higher moral and social principles. However, as the truest of all religions, Christianity should produce people with consistent, loving behavior, in speech and deed toward those around them.

Thus, for James, Christianity is the "religion that is pure and undefiled before God." He assumes that all other religions were contaminated to a greater or lesser degree. The true teaching of a religion and the moral practices of its adherents should converge where people notice those suffering in their communities—like the widows and orphans (the most prevalent examples of the economically neglected in the ancient world)— and where they take time to encourage the deprived with words and to comfort them with food and clothing. It's not that social concerns should occupy 100 percent of a religion's, or of Christianity's, agenda. Rather, sacrificial concern and activity for the suffering points back to the truth quality of its teaching. If Christianity, then, has the truest teaching, this should be patently observable even by nonadherents as Christians give to others in need.

James's focus on "orphans and widows" as the objects of social concern follows a well-worn path laid down by laws and prophetic sermons in the Old Testament. These most helpless of Israel's citizens stood at the mercy of their communities with little way of earning a livelihood and no legal standing. Thus Deuteronomy provided that they should take their fill from a full tithe (10 percent) of the stored produce of Israel (14:28–29), that they should not be "deprive[d]" (24:17). Prophets steadily warned Israel about its mistreatment of orphans and widows (Jer. 5:28; Ezek. 22:7; Zech. 7:10). Isaiah 1:10–17 specifically condemned Israel for observing the rites of Jewish religion while disregarding the orphans and widows in their midst.

The closing admonition "to keep oneself unstained by the world" assumes that Christians are involved with the people in their communities in speech and action. Such involvement may hide a potential danger. Moral lapses and sinful temptations may well be encountered when relating to people who are not believers. The word *world* is not a neutral word in the New Testament. Rather, it is, as here, an antagonist to Christianity, almost universally associated with sin. It is where believers have left their former ways of life and is what sirens them to leave their new life in Christ. So, James warned believers to be vigilant in maintaining their moral virtue as they involved themselves in the lives of those around them, because the ones to whom they minister remain enamored by the world and its hold on them.

Both the speech and the social action of believers, then, are evidence for the truth quality of the gospel. They are essential tools of evangelism, or perhaps more appropriately of "pre-evangelism," to draw people to the truth and the incalculable positive impact Christianity can have on their lives and those in the world around them.

SERMON

Listening Well and Doing Good

(James 1:19–27)

Better or bitter. Tough times and tempting circumstances will make you one or the other. Just because one is a Christian does not mean that he or she will automatically be better after an ordeal. What one becomes through trial and temptation is determined by one's attitude and actions following the tough times. The problem, as I see it, is our desire to have an explanation for everything. We Christians want to know the "who, what, when, where, why, and how" of our tough times. When we cannot discover an acceptable answer to those questions, we often find ourselves struggling with poor attitudes and pitiful actions.

The challenge then is to become better, to mature and grow through the tough experiences of life. Such maturity comes through two responses.

Developing the Right Attitude (1:19–21)

When things go wrong in our lives, we first begin to look for who or what is at fault. Very often the real answer is: No one is at fault. This is true because life is not fair. Bad things happen to good people. That's just the way it is! The response to such injustice is varied. Sometimes we choose to stop listening; sometimes we choose to stop caring; sometimes we choose to vent our anger at God and everyone else in our lives.

James again offered his readers wise counsel. James 1:19 reads, "let everyone be quick to listen, slow to speak, slow to anger." Perhaps no single verse in all of this epistle transcends time and generations more than these few words. This advice is as relevant in the twenty-first century as it was in the first. As a matter of fact, these few words, when put into practice, will take you far down the path toward spiritual maturity. Consider the value of this proverbial statement.

Be Quick to Listen

Be eager to hear the wisdom of others. Such eagerness begins with the word of God. Everything we need for developing spiritual maturity is contained in the scriptures. The Word provides advice on: attitudes, marriage, parenting, working relationships, friendship, worship, work, leisure, materialism, benevolence, and the list goes on. Listen carefully to what God has to say.

Trusted friends and family members also provide wise counsel. Listen to Proverbs 27:17 from the NIV: "As iron sharpens iron, so one man sharpens another." Listen to those who love you; they truly want to help. They don't deserve your blame; they deserve your ears!

Be Slow to Speak

Preachers are notorious for talking profusely. We think we need to have an answer or comment for everything. I've learned through the years that such verbose responses are not necessarily good. In talking too much, one may just say something he or she hasn't thought of yet! I've also learned that I seldom have to apologize for something I didn't say. As a child, my parents would read to me at bedtime. (Dad would often fall asleep in the process.) I still remember one of the first poems I ever learned from those bedtime readings.

A wise old owl sat upon an oak,
The more he saw, the less he spoke;
The less he spoke, the more he heard.
Why aren't we like that wise old bird?[1]

I think James would have liked that poem. Be slow to speak and quick to hear, and you will save yourself much grief.

Be Slow to Anger

James expanded at some length on the third facet of this proverb. Obviously, this is the most challenging portion of the quest for most. Uncontrolled anger works against the righteous life that God desires for us. Angrily blaming others often leads to other moral issues and evil choices that take us farther away from God, not closer. Case in point: In 2001 Thomas Junta was convicted of involuntary manslaughter at his son's hockey practice. The entire episode—the fight with another father, the subsequent death, and now the manslaughter conviction—all grew out of a fit of uncontrolled anger. Two families will never be the same again. Four children will have to grow up without a dad, and another family will endure the pain and embarrassment of Junta's actions and prison absence. The irony of this whole angry affair is incredible: Junta's complaint that sparked the confrontation was that this practice was to be a "no contact" scrimmage and that his son had been elbowed in the face by another player.[2]

Remember: Anger will lead to other sins, not to righteous behavior. Learning to cope with anger will require much more than just counting to ten before you take action. Most of the time that simple exercise just delays the inevitable for about ten seconds! When you discover that your anger is getting the best of you, take time to read the Word. Few of us are able to have a Bible present at all times, so let me suggest an alternative. Fill both sides of a 3x5 card with Bible verses that have been the most inspiring for your life. Keep that card in your purse or pocket. When you feel the steam of anger beginning to build, take the card out and read it. It is difficult to "explode" when you are reading passages of God's inspiration. It certainly is not a cure-all, but it will make a difference. And it sure beats counting to ten!

Developing the Right Actions (1:22–27)

James addressed two separate courses of action. The first is to take an honest look inside and respond accordingly. It is a self-evaluation exercise that must precede the second course of action.

Remembering One's Reflection (1:22–25)

Have you ever considered how often you see your reflection in a mirror on a daily basis? Count the number of mirrors in your house, your place of employment, and the mall where you shop. You may be surprised how often your face is staring back at you. We shuffle out of bed at dawn's early light, only to be greeted by our reflection in the bathroom mirror, and it's not a pretty sight. We then proceed to work hard in front of that mirror to make our image presentable for the day ahead. Throughout the day we stop to check our hair, teeth, makeup, and smiles in the many mirrors around us. If that isn't enough, our image is probably one of the last visions we see just prior to retiring for the night. We are confronted with the reflection of our image so many times each day that it is inconceivable that any person could forget what he or she looks like. James compared such an absurd forgetfulness to the person who hears the word of God and yet does nothing about it.

Verse 25 refers to the "law of liberty," called the "royal law" in 2:8. The Gospels refer to it as the Great (or Greatest) Commandment (Mt. 22:36, 38). In his conversation with the rich young ruler, Jesus encouraged the ruler to "love your neighbor as yourself" (Mt. 19:19). Loving one's neighbor is not an option in the Christian life. It is putting one's faith into action. Right actions always follow right attitudes, but right attitudes without the right actions are empty.

We must be quick to listen but also quick to act. Hearing without doing, James says, is unacceptable. We are deluding ourselves if we believe we just have to listen well. The next time you look into the mirror, ask yourself this question, "Have I acted upon what I've heard?"

Remembering One's Religion (1:26–27)

This word *religion* should be understood as "the outward expression of religion in ritual and liturgy and ceremony."[3]

James was concerned that the person caught up in the ritual and ceremony of religion (like reading the right books, singing the right songs, and going through the right motions) could be deceived into believing that God is pleased. James then directed his readers to "religion that is pure and undefiled" by specifically denoting three areas of action that are important to God:

1. Exercising Control of the Tongue

   James would have much more to say about this later in his letter, but he took this opportunity to reflect on his proverbial statement, "be...slow to speak." The mark of a true Christian is not the capacity to communicate with the tongue but the ability to control the tongue.

   "The boneless tongue, so small and weak,
   Can crush and kill," declares the Greek.

"The tongue destroys a greater horde,"
The Turk asserts, "than does the sword."
The Persian proverb wisely saith,
"A lengthy tongue—an early death."
Or sometimes takes this form instead,
"Don't let your tongue cut off your head."
"The tongue can speak a word whose speed,"
Say the Chinese, "outstrips the steed."
The Arab sages said in part,
"The tongue's great storehouse is the heart."
From Hebrew was the maxim sprung,
"Thy feet should slip, but ne'er the tongue."
The sacred writer crowns the whole,
"Who keep the tongue doth keep his soul."[4]

2. Exercising Compassion for Those in Need

James specifically mentioned widows and orphans in distress. The orphans and widows were the most helpless people in Jewish society. The law and the prophets spoke to those who mistreated the widows and orphans and promised severe consequences (Jer. 5:28; Ezek. 22:7; Zech. 7:10). One of Jesus' three resurrection miracles was to restore the life of an only son to a widow from Nain (Lk. 7:11–17). If we are to be truly "religious," we must move from the comfort of our pews to address the pain of those in need.

3. Exercising Conviction to Live an Unpolluted Life

Pollution has become a genuine concern in today's culture. Factories and businesses are monitored to insure that they are not guilty of polluting the air, water, or soil. Research is progressing toward an alternate, cleaner fuel to replace the fossil fuels for our transportation needs. Households are encouraged to recycle to eliminate unnecessary waste. As we leave no stone unturned to solve pollution problems, we have overlooked the biggest rock in the road—personal pollution. From a spiritual standpoint, we have forgotten that our lives must parallel our speech. No one will be interested in listening to what we have to say about God if our actions do not reflect what we say. Has your inner life and visible witness become a polluted landfill? Perhaps you have some cleaning up to do. James 1:27 reminds us, "Religion that is pure and undefiled before God, the Father, is this: to care for orphans and widows in their distress, and to keep oneself unstained by the world."

How does the believer accomplish all of this? It is not easy nor does it happen (overnight). It is, however, possible, and it all begins when everyone is "quick to listen, slow to speak, [and] slow to anger."

Chapter 3

Loving the Outcast
James 2:1–13

Exegesis

James 2 expands on the theme of hearing the word of God. James developed the theme briefly in 1:22–25, after introducing it in the three-part proverb in 1:19, "Be quick to listen." The second chapter exposes the hypocrisy of those who say they hear God's word but discriminate against the poor. It also serves notice that such violations of the supreme command to love one's neighbor do not go unnoticed in God's judgment. In 1:27 James defined "religion that is pure and undefiled before God." The hypothetical example and chastizement of the readers in 2:1–13 demonstrates what pure religion is not: favoring the rich over the helpless and being influenced by the world's attitudes rather than God's.

Looking Past the Superficial (2:1–4)

Sizing people up by how they look was as common in New Testament times as it is today. Humans quite naturally assess other people by observing such things as the cut of their clothes, the label on their jeans, the style of their hair, the fluency of their speech, and the expression on their face. Our visual senses, based on exterior factors alone, so easily transmit perceptions of people. Our positive as well as our negative "first impressions" quickly lead us astray. An even bigger problem is that God does not determine a person's value in this way. We know this because Jesus did not treat people this way. As those who hear God's Word and who are committed to Christ as Lord, we should try to look at people as God does.

The NRSV and *New Living Translation* (NLT) stand alone in phrasing 2:1 as a question. The imperative mood of the Greek verb is preferred and makes more sense in the context, and a minister will do well to read several English translations before preparing a sermon on it.

The NRSV's "acts of favoritism" (2:1) translates a compound Greek word literally meaning "receiving the face." In the Old Testament the equivalent Hebrew word is applied to personal relationships as well as administration of civil justice. Leviticus 19:15 (see also Ps. 82:2; Prov. 18:5) instructs the people of Israel, "You shall not be partial to the poor or defer to the great," and Deuteronomy 1:17 instructs judges within each tribe, "You must not be partial in judging: hear out the small and the great alike." The basis for this instruction, as Deuteronomy 10:17 explains, is that God "is not partial." The New Testament uses the Greek word translated here, and related words, to underline God's nature. Romans 2:11 states quite tersely, "For God shows no partiality." God's impartiality is a formative principle in acceptance of Gentiles, such as Cornelius, who receive the gospel (Acts 10:34); in judgment of Jews and Gentiles for their sinful rebellion (Rom. 2:11); in support for Paul's gospel message (Gal.2:6); in keeping a watchful eye on how Christian masters treat their slaves (Eph. 6:9); and on how Christian slaves obey their masters (Col. 3:25).

Rather than appealing to the character of God, James's initial appeal is to the readers as fellow Christians committed to Christ. He stresses his commitment and relationship to his readers by using the Greek word for "brothers," translated in NRSV as "brothers and sisters" (1:2; 2:1; 2:5, 14; 3:1, 10, 12; 4:11; 5:19) or "beloved" (5:7, 9, 10, 12), and left untranslated (1:16, 19)—as a rhetorical device to begin this new section, something he does routinely. The New Testament uses this word frequently to refer to Christians, reflecting our common relationship to God, as sons and daughters, as well as our sibling relationship to Christ as first-born son.

The last phrase, "in our glorious Lord Jesus Christ," anchors the appeal for impartiality. Its impact is especially weighty because it is the only place, other than the salutation in 1:1, in which James employs the term "Jesus Christ." So it must be deemed important to include it here. The importance is underlined by the addition of "Lord" and "glorious" to "Jesus Christ" in the Greek. James wanted his readers to get the strong impact of the truth: "favoritism" and "Jesus Christ" do not go together. One other detail adds further weight to the argument. Of the fourteen times James uses the term "Lord," only five of these refer to Jesus (1:1; 2:1; 5:7, 8, 14 and possibly 5:15). Two of these speak expectantly of Christ's coming in judgment (5:7, 8; compare 5:9). This suggests that James wanted his readers to view their "favoritism" in light of Christ's impartial judgment.

The placement of the Greek word for "glory" after Christ is especially odd if it is intended as an adjective, as most translations agree. Technically, it can be interpreted as modifying "Jesus Christ," ("glorious Jesus Christ") or "Lord" ("Jesus Christ, Lord of glory"). Or it can be taken to stand alone, further highlighting Jesus Christ as "the glory" ("Jesus Christ, the glory"). Its placement at the end slightly favors the latter, though it is a bit awkward to translate into English. The term "glory" in the New Testament when referring to Christ often connects to his resurrection, highlighting how he came to be Lord, but that would seem to come out of the blue in this context. In the Old Testament, glory commonly refers to the presence of God. Such a deft reference to Christ as the manifestation of God's presence seems more compatible with the emphasis here on impartiality. This interpretation is reinforced by the reference to Christ as Lord and Judge upon his return in 5:7–9. "Glory" is best recognized, then, as signifying the presence of God as judge.

James 2:2–4 showcases the kind of favoritism the author believed was going on in the churches. Despite its vividness, the story is hypothetical, exaggerating certain details to contrast starkly the two unknown visitors to the assembly. The first visitor is at the very upper echelon of society, not just rich but powerful, adorned by a gold ring and a "shining" (NRSV–"fine"), probably white, maybe brand new, toga picturing the typical attire of a Roman nobleman or politician of high rank. The second visitor's clothing is not just shabby but filthy. Both body and clothes remain unwashed because this impoverished person has no change of clothes. Picture a homeless person living on the street in contemporary, urban America. Church members catching a first glimpse of the two visitors are thrilled and honored to have the first one sit in the adjoining seat. But the second is ushered to an inconspicuous place or told to sit on the floor where every action can be closely monitored.

James did not accuse just one person of this kind of blatant favoritism. He castigates the entire fellowship of believers for taking unwarranted actions based on superficial assessments of people. The second person pronouns are plural as are all the verbs referring to the interaction with the two visitors. It's as if James is saying that he could enter any church he wrote or knew about and the same thing would happen. Every one of the believers in every fellowship would all do the same thing. And it's not just about where you allow people to sit. It's about how people are being treated on innumerable matters. This teaching applies not just to visitors, but also to fellow believers in the churches. The believers allowed superficial, worldly criteria to determine who were the worst of people and who were the best of people. James labels this as stemming from evil influence. He condemned it as counterproductive to the fellowship of believers.

This is the only place in the New Testament that uses the Greek word *synagogue* ("assembly," v. 2) for a Christian gathering. Normally, this word signifies the gathering of Jews who began meeting in homes and synagogue buildings throughout Israel and the Roman world some time before 200 B.C.E. Early Christians, at least those with whom James was familiar, followed the Jewish pattern in their assemblies for Bible study, fellowship, and the Lord's Supper.

Remembering Your Own Exploited Status (2:5–7)

James reminded his readers of their identity. He uses economic and social terms to do so. In a world with no middle class (a product of the industrial age), where the very few, mostly landowners, were rich, almost everybody was grouped as poor, having to live from day to day, never having expendable, discretionary resources. With few exceptions, Christians were poor. A rich visitor brought excitement. A rich member brought hope for help for the majority of members. They were not poor because they were Christians. They were poor simply because they were like everyone else. As such, socially and economically, Christians stood at the mercy of the rich and powerful, as did the rest of the poor. Coddling the rich and despising the poor worked against their own interests and identity. It also ignored the spiritual issues involved in valuing or devaluing people for superficial reasons.

The use of "brothers and sisters" in 2:5 signals a slight shift in emphasis. It also seeks to shake its readers to attention with the opening command to "listen" (remember 1:19). These early Christians were deluding themselves into thinking the way they did before they believed in Jesus. This had to stop. Their actions were a discredit to the poor (including themselves), to the Christian faith to which they were devoted, and to their own local body of believers with whom they were united.

The principles imbedded in the searing question posed in 2:5 come right out of Christ's own teaching, which in turn was imbedded in Old Testament teaching. "Blessed are you who are poor,/ for yours is the kingdom of God" (Lk. 6:20; compare Matt. 5:3). "Better to be poor and walk in integrity /than to be crooked in one's ways even though rich" (Prov. 28:6; compare Job 34:25–29; Prov. 14:31). The overlap between poverty and piety can also be seen in Isaiah 61:1, in which preaching good news to the "oppressed" assumes all humanity is spiritually impoverished and in need of a hopeful message from God. When questioned as to whether he was truly the Messiah (Lk. 7:20), Jesus said he himself fulfilled the Isaiah passage. Paul was clearly aware that believers usually met in the larger homes of the richer members. Still, in 1 Corinthians 1:26–28, he acknowledged that most believers were not among the social and economic elite. He went even further and claimed that this was a spiritual benefit for them, something James 1:9–11 had assumed earlier.

A contrast appears in the Greek of 2:6. "The poor" is singular in Greek, while "the rich" is plural. This indicates that James is not referring to the rich man in the story of the two visitors, but to rich people in general. The dramatic accusation forces readers to plead guilty to favoritism against really poor individuals who have crossed their paths. It also telescopes out to remind them of incidents in their own lives when the elite have exploited them. Three questions follow the accusation. The questions list social crimes of the rich and powerful against their communities in their hunger for money and power. The poor believers should not be so quick to forget.

The first question paints the general picture of oppression and exploitation, common both then and now. The powerful always have the rest of the community at a disadvantage. The poor masses are always dependent on the few rich for jobs to feed their families. The rich power the local economy. This reality is impossible to avoid. What is open for change is how the powerful leverage their position—for themselves only or for others in the community. This makes all the difference. In general, the situation was not good, as James sought to remind his readers.

The second question, posed so dramatically with the term "drag," specifies one way the powerful tend to use their economic and social position to get what they want legally. What is pictured is not criminal court but civil court, probably involving property rights and debt payment. The best biblical example of this is Jezebel's conniving efforts to obtain Naboth's vineyard for Ahab in 1 Kings 21. In every community, the powerful are better acquainted with the law, and probably with the judges as well. They know how to work the system against everyone else, especially the powerless poor. James assumes his readers had personal experience with the long arm of the powerful.

The third question focuses on the damage the powerful inflict on James's readers as Christians and on the Christ in whom they believe. The term "the excellent name" certainly refers to Jesus Christ, specifically to "Jesus," whose name was "invoked over" the early Christians as they were baptized. The injury in mind could be insults the rich scornfully hurl at Christians, possibly mocking their belief in Jesus' resurrection or his claims to be God's Son. However, in this context, what may have been in mind is the bad name Jesus received in the community when his followers were charged in court by the powerful. A significant doctrinal statement is implied here. James calls the acts or words of the powerful "blasphemy." In the Jewish context as evident in the Old Testament, blasphemy normally was a crime of contempt or disrespect toward God. James's claim that the name of Jesus was being blasphemed assumes Christian belief in the divinity of Christ.

Honor the Law of Love by Not Discriminating (2:8–11)

James clinches his case against his readers by explaining that their favoritism and discrimination violates God's law in the Hebrew Scriptures. Neither they nor we can escape his indictment.

James expects that his readers will be chagrined when they realize that their attitudes and behavior have broken the Jewish law. Such focus on the Jewish law suggests that most of his original readers, if not all, were Jewish Christians. Still, all Christians then and now recognize our dependence on Jewish Scripture and Jewish law if we are to know God's law and apply it to everyone.

James quoted the law of neighbor love from Leviticus 19:18, but calling it "the royal law" suggests that James interpreted it on the basis of Jesus' kingdom teaching. Jesus made love of neighbor the signature law on which Christian and human behavior ought to be assessed. Jesus' teaching in this regard is prominent not only in the gospels (Mt. 5:43; 19:19; 22:37–40; Mk. 12:31, 33; Lk. 10:27), but also in Paul (Rom. 13:9; Gal. 5:14). In fact, Leviticus 19:18 is the Old Testament passage most often quoted in the New Testament (nine times). Jesus raised this principle from obscurity as one of hundreds of principles in Jewish law and teaching, to its preeminent position, where it stands today, inside and outside Christian teaching.

The law of neighbor love is not like a normal law. People cannot be prosecuted for not loving others. However, we can assess and regulate ourselves with this principle. When incorporated as a life principle, it helps promote healthy, helpful behavior. It functions as a freeing, positive internal principle. For this reason, which becomes clearer in 2:12, James appears to consider "the perfect law, the law of liberty" in 1:25, and "the royal law," in 2:8, to be the same law, the law of neighbor love.

James argues his case essentially by unfolding a syllogism: Partiality is to neighbor love as one law is to the whole law, as also murder or adultery is to the whole law. Violation of the first means violation of the second because in each case the first is part of the second. This is important to see because James does not consider neighbor love to be merely one of many equal statutes of the law. It is not an ascending syllogism: partiality to neighbor love to the whole law. Rather, neighbor love is equal to the whole law. Neighbor love encompasses the entire law's essence, as we see in Jesus' answer to the rich young ruler (Lk. 18:22).

James 2:9 (and 2:11) describes those guilty of partiality as "transgressors"; some translations say "lawbreakers." It can signify someone who has stepped over a boundary, like a trespasser. Paul is the only other New Testament writer to use the original Greek word (Rom. 2:25, 27; Gal. 2:18). The word places people in a category—sinners. Once in the category, they cannot break out apart from Christ. For Paul, every human being is a "transgressor" of the law. Though he does not make such an explicit statement, James would apparently agree. Both Paul and James assume that people in this category deserve and will receive God's judgment. Discriminating or showing favoritism is a disgraceful act that puts even believers in this category in terms of how they are presently acting. This goes against their commitment to God and expectations summarized in the royal law of loving one's neighbor.

The principle that breaking one law makes one a transgressor of all law, specifically expressed in 2:10, anchors James's indictment. This is not an idea he conjures up. First-century Jewish teachers often articulated the idea. James assumed his readers agreed that breaking one law makes one guilty of breaking the entire law. James wanted the readers to apply this truism to themselves and see how guilty they were. Today, we, too, paint murderers or thieves, who may have committed only one crime, with a similar broad brush, categorizing them as "criminals," social outcasts who are not to be trusted in any regard. Too seldom do we paint ourselves with the broad brush of guilt because we have played favorites, playing up to the rich and powerful and ignoring the poor and needy.

James 2:11 picks up two of the examples from the Ten Commandments—adultery and murder (Ex. 20:13–15; Deut. 5:17–19). Jesus did the same when he quizzed the rich young ruler (Mt. 19:18–19). Their different ordering results from James using the Septuagint version while Matthew used the Hebrew version of the Old Testament. James could have chosen any Old Testament law to make his point. However, these two are particularly heinous and notorious in terms of transgressing clear borders sanctified by God—marriage and human creation.

Behave Mercifully toward Your Neighbor (2:12–13)

James concludes his argument against discrimination by voicing a life principle. He grounds the principle in the law of neighbor love, now called "the law of liberty," as in 1:25. He also supplies both a stick and a carrot to get us to implement this principle in our lives so that we may face God's judgment with confidence.

What stands out in 2:12 is the repetition of the little word *so* before both "speak" and "act." The Greek word could be rendered "in this way," or "like this." We tend much too easily to think of our moral and spiritual life, and so our Christian life, as a series of actions. James shows his great concern about our personal speech ethics by bracketing out our speech from our actions. Speech is not a minor, inconsequential part of Christian ethics. It is as an equal and parallel concern with acts. Just as we must apply the law of neighbor love to our actions, so, too, must we apply it to our speech. Our speaking and acting each require premeditated decisions motivated by our love for others. Having already made such decisions in love, we won't discriminate toward the powerful or against the powerless. Neither will we speak ill of others nor lie about the truth. We will not physically assault others or steal from them.

Christ has freed believers from condemnation by the law. The New Testament does teach that everyone, including Christians, will stand before Christ's judgment seat. At that time

Christ, on God's behalf, will assesses the lives of every individual. Second Corinthians 5:10 articulates this principle best when it says: "For all of us must appear before the judgment seat of Christ, so that each may receive recompense for what has been done in the body, whether good or evil." James was not alone in believing that Christians will receive varying levels of reward–as well as possible condemnation–should their lives be so out of sync with their Christian commitment as to render it void.

James strikes us with a heavy "stick": Believers who characteristically do not show mercy will receive no mercy at the judgment. They will be condemned and separated out from the saved. Here James reminds us of Jesus' teaching in the story of the sheep and the goats: "As you did it to one of the least of these who are members of my family, you did it to me" (Mt. 25:40).

James's "carrot" states simply: "Mercy triumphs over judgment" (v. 13). Imitating God by acting and speaking to others with graciousness gives us a ticket to pass through judgment, confident of being one of Christ's sheep. Judgment, then, becomes nothing to fear. It is a victory celebration. Human appearances may weigh unduly on us in our interactions with people, but they don't with God. This was good news for most of James's readers, who numbered among the poor. It is also good news for those of us today who number among the wealthy, for Christ will not hold that against us either. Rather, he cares how we transfer the fruit of loving our neighbor from the church's teaching into our daily lives.

SERMON

Love and the Unlovely

(James 2:1–17)

James is a good storyteller. I like the way he weaves his hypothetical narratives into the fabric of his spiritual lessons. His stories paint a mental image to which we can all relate. The story of chapter two is no exception. These images hit close to home for the body of Christ in any age, but especially for the church of this superficial twenty-first century.

A Royal Crime (2:1–7)

With a single glance, we size up those we meet and immediately begin to draw some conclusions. The man who drives a new luxury car is viewed with more respect than the guy who cruises around in an eight-year-old compact. The woman who looks like she just stepped out of the pages of a fashion catalogue always draws more attention than the woman in jeans pushing a stroller. Based on what we see, we make assumptions that may not be valid. For instance, the guy in the luxury auto may be stressed to the max because he is up to his eyeballs in debt, while the driver of the compact is debt free and enjoys a relaxing life. To discover that additional information changes our perspective quickly. Things are not always what they seem to be.

As Christians we must get beyond the superficial. It is not the outward appearance that tells the story; the real truth comes from within. After God rejected Saul as king in Israel, he sent Samuel to Bethlehem, to the household of Jesse, to anoint a new king. Jesse brought out his oldest son, Eliab, and the wise Samuel was impressed. "Surely the LORD's anointed is now before the LORD," he exclaimed in 1 Samuel 16:6. But this was not God's choice, so he interrupted Samuel, "Do not look on his appearance or on the height of his stature, because I have rejected him; for the LORD *does not see as mortals see*; they look on the outward appearance, but the LORD looks on the heart" (1 Sam. 16:7, italics by author).

Six more impressive sons paraded past the aging judge, but Samuel was not allowed to anoint any of them. You can almost sense the exasperation in Samuel's voice, "'Are these all the sons you have?' 'There is still the youngest,' Jesse answered, 'but he is tending the sheep'" (v. 11, NIV). You can hear the apologetic tone in Jesse's voice. Samuel wanted to see this young shepherd boy, so Jesse sent for him. When David arrived, God revealed to Samuel that this young boy was the one he should anoint (v. 12). Everyone's last pick was God's first choice. David was to become known as the "man after [God's] own heart" (1 Sam. 13:14; Acts 13:22). Things are not always what they seem to be.

The problem James addressed here is an outgrowth of our infatuation with the superficial. This story is hypothetical, but James may have witnessed a similar incident of favoritism.

The scene is easy to picture. Two men walk into the church gathering about the same time, but one glance would indicate that they did not arrive together. The one man, obviously wealthy, nearly glows from all of his gold and the new, extra white tunic he wears. To the assembly of Christians this might have been an unusual sight since history indicates that the majority of first-century church members came from the working or slave class. The crowd parts like the Red Sea as this powerful individual makes his way to the front. There he is presented with the best seat in the house. (Times sure have changed—today, the back pew is the most sought after seat in the house!) You can see the wheels in the minds of the elders working overtime: "Treat this guy well; we will need him for next year's capital gifts campaign."

The other visitor is completely overlooked. No wonder! Not only is he poor, but he has the odor of one who has not bathed recently. He, too, is unique to the church but at the opposite end of the spectrum from Mr. Glitz-and-glitter. Finally, the head deacon, Demetrius, notices this vagrant who has wandered into their assembly and curtly shuffles him off to some obscure corner where their royal guest won't see or smell him.

Just thinking of the hypothetical situation made James livid with righteous indignation. In the heart of God no soul appreciates or depreciates based on his or her exterior. Jesus died for the poor and the rich, the handsome and homely, the loveable and the unlovely. How can the church be so superficial?

I remember hearing about a preacher who disguised himself as a homeless man. Wearing faded, disheveled clothes and smelling less than pleasant, he entered the church building foyer one Sunday morning as the other parishioners were arriving. The good church folks basically ignored him and tried to stay upwind of where he was standing. After several awkward moments in the foyer, he ventured into the worship center and sat down. No one shared his pew, so he sat alone through the song service. Finally, the worship team sat down in preparation for the morning message. A long pause ensued as the congregation began to look for the preacher. He finally stood up, removed his hat and beard, and made his way to the pulpit. The congregation was in shock, as you can imagine, but it did make for a memorable introduction to his sermon on this text in James!

Our culture is enamored with those who possess wealth and fame. Multiple magazines and television shows are devoted to the lives of the rich and famous. When it comes to meeting a sports icon or film star, fans will step way out of their comfort zones to shake a hand or to get an autograph, acting in ways they would never consider in a "normal" setting. The paparazzi can afford to make themselves a nuisance because their pictures of the popular elite will always have a market in our star struck culture. Even those in the church are not exempt from being caught up in the excitement of it all. Why are we so influenced by the superficial?

In his book *Kingdoms in Conflict,* Charles Colson wrote about his time with the Nixon administration and a strategic plan he devised to cultivate political allies. In short, he brought key leaders to the White House, where they were wined and dined, exposed to key leaders in the administration, and given the opportunity to meet the President. Though prearranged by Colson, the visits to the Oval Office were made to seem spontaneous. President Nixon would visit warmly with the guests and then present each leader with a set of gold plated cuff links embossed with the president seal. By the end of the evening, even the most ardent skeptic had become an ally of the President. Mr. Colson observed:

> Ironically, none were more compliant than the religious leaders. Of all people, they should have been the most aware of our sinful nature and the least overwhelmed by pomp and protocol. But theological knowledge sometimes wilts in the face of worldly power.[1]

It is true. We, of all people, should know better than to let the razzle-dazzle of fame take us in. Since God looks at the heart, that would be a good place for us to start. We would do well to get rid of every hint of favoritism and to distinguish the genuine from the superficial.

A Royal Command

James provides us with some wisdom on how we might avoid falling over ourselves for the rich and famous.

Be Loving (2:8–9)

Humorist Dave Barry writes,

> Love can be wonderful, but it also can be destructive. It can cause people to lie, to cheat, to commit murder, and—worst of all—to write lyrics like these: "Why do birds suddenly appear, Every time you are near?" These lyrics are, of course, from the Carpenters' huge hit "Close to You." You frankly have to ask yourself: "Do I really want to be near somebody who causes birds to appear suddenly? Didn't Alfred Hitchcock do a horror movie about this?"[2]

Our pop culture writes, composes, creates, and sings about love; but I am not sure it understands the meaning of true love. Apart from God's perspective, love is often confused with feel-good but empty emotions. True love is seeking the best for those around us. It is putting the needs of others ahead of our own wants or needs. Love is not dependent upon the emotions. It is a decision of the mind and will. Culturally speaking, love is a feeling that is more beneficial for the giver than the recipient. Spiritually speaking, love is an intentional sacrifice of one's feelings to meet the needs of others.

A missionary was once asked, "What pay do you receive for the hardships you undergo and the sacrifices you make, living and working among these people?" The missionary took from his pocket a letter from one of his students, worn with much handling, and read two sentences, "But for you, I would not have known Jesus Christ, our savior. Every morning I kneel before God and thank God for you." "That," the missionary responded, "is my pay." Such is the power of godly love, and that kind of love breaks down the barriers of favoritism.[3]

Be Obedient (2:10–11)

Most of us tend to be rather smug about our own goodness. If we are not guilty of some heinous crime, if we love our families, and if we don't kick the pet dog, then we usually think we are better than average. James offers another perspective. He reminds us that to fail in one small aspect of law-keeping is to be as guilty as if we had broken every command that God has issued since the beginning of time. It is true that the temporal and social consequences of sin differ greatly. A lustful look is trivial compared to mass murder. Still, it is important for every Christian to understand that in God's eyes you are as guilty as the worst criminal on death row. One tiny transgression will separate you from God as easily as a multitude of sins. The eternal consequence of sin is the same for all. Consequently, you have no right to be conceited and superficial. We are all in the same boat. As the old hymn goes, we are "sinking deep in sin, far from the peaceful shore."[4] When you truly realize that we are all in the same condition, you are less likely to show favoritism.

Whenever you face the temptation to use superficial reasons to treat one person differently from another, just remember: How a believer lives is a reflection of his or her relationship with the Creator. God calls us to righteous obedience because obedience matters. We will not earn heavenly bonus points by our submission to God's authority, but we will be credible witnesses in the eyes of a watching world. The postmodern mind is searching for that which is real and genuine, not plastic. What does the postmodern person see in your life?

Be Merciful (2:12–13)

"Mercy triumphs" (v. 13). Jimmy Allen, minister and former president of the Southern Baptist Convention wrote, "The first man in history to reach out and voluntarily touch lepers didn't die of leprosy. He died at the hands of religious leaders who wouldn't have touched a leper on a bet."[5]

Jesus was the greatest living example of what it means to be merciful. Mercy is not getting what we deserve. If a police officer stops you for speeding and all you receive is a warning, that is mercy. You did not get what you deserved.

Mercy is part of the character of God. When Moses asked to see God's glory, God replied: "I will make all my goodness pass before you, and will proclaim before you the name, 'The LORD'; and I will be gracious to whom I will be gracious, and will show mercy on whom I will show mercy" (Ex. 33:19).

Time and time again throughout history we witness the mercy of God. In mercy God demonstrated incredible patience to the grumbling nation of Israel as they journeyed through the wilderness on their way to the Promised Land. In mercy God provided a continual supply of flour and oil to the Gentile widow of Zarephath so that she, her son, and the prophet Elijah could survive the famine (1 Kings 17:10–15). The mercy of God fills the pages of scripture.

From saving a host the embarrassment of running out of wine at a wedding feast (Jn. 2:1–11) to restoring his dear friend Lazarus' life after four days in the tomb (Jn. 11:1–44), Jesus' ministry was characterized by acts and words of mercy.

He simply fulfilled the prophet Micah's definition of true religion:

> He has showed you, O man, what is good.
> And what does the LORD require of you?
> To act justly and to love mercy
> and to walk humbly with your God.
>
> (Mic. 6:8, NIV)

This definition transcends time and generations.

Perhaps no godly trait points others to Jesus better than our acts of mercy. James knew that and encouraged the church of all ages to be a genuine reflection of our merciful God in our words and deeds. God has extended mercy to you. Now it is your turn: Be merciful to those around you. You never know when your acts of mercy may truly change another's life.

In the movie *Seabiscuit* Tom Smith is a broken-down, unemployed cowboy. Millionaire Charles Howard is looking for just the right person to be the new trainer for his horse racing enterprise. As they talk around the campfire, Howard notices that Smith is nursing an old, seemingly worn-out horse with a broken leg. Howard asks why.

Tom replies, "You don't throw a whole life away just 'cause it's banged up a bit." Every horse is good for something, Tom claims. He gets the job.

Together they search for just the right horse. Finally, they buy an unlikely prospect, Seabiscuit. The horse has a temperament that makes it an unlikely prospect for racing success, but through Smith's patience the horse improves.

Tom hires a second-rate jockey named John "Red" Pollard to ride Seabiscuit. At 5'7", Red is considered too tall to be anything but a bush-league jockey, but there is an immediate, almost mystical connection between Pollard and Seabiscuit.

Red's size is not the only issue; he is blind in one eye, a fact he has concealed from everyone. During a crucial race at Santa Anita, Red's limited vision allows a competing horse, Rosemont, to overtake Seabiscuit on Red's blind side, beating Seabiscuit in the closing seconds of the race.

Tom Smith is outraged that the jockey failed to urge Seabiscuit to keep the winning pace. He presses the jockey to explain how he could possibly let something so elementary happen in this important race. Finally, in a burst of emotion, Red admits he's blind in one eye.

Tom angrily urges Mr. Howard to fire Red; but, to his surprise, Mr. Howard requests that Red remain as his jockey. Tom demands a reason, and Mr. Howard responds simply, "You don't throw away a whole life just because it's banged up a bit."[6]

James shows us what it takes to be different from the rest of the world. Anyone can be superficial and show favoritism, but the genuine disciple of Jesus strives to be loving, to be obedient, and to be merciful. What strides will you make in these directions this week?

CHAPTER 4

Doing What You Believe

JAMES 2:14–26

Exegesis

James continues to expand on what it truly means to hear the word of God with an eye toward what was said about doing the word in 1:22–25. The focus moves from decrying discrimination and lobbying for neighbor love as a life principle to the theological issue of how faith and works relate to all of this. In a very real sense hypocrisy is still at issue when people say they are believers but don't act like believers, not even seeking to incorporate neighbor love into their daily interactions with others. Now, with mastery and force, James convinces us that our faith in God and our trust in Jesus must work in tandem with our behavior or it is not really faith at all. Faith and works are two sides of the same coin. Three times in this passage (vv. 17, 20, 26), the message is repeated: Faith without works is dead! By this James clearly means that such empty "faith" is not saving faith either. It is no more than mouthing words.

Workless Faith Is No Faith (2:14–17)

James opens with two rhetorical questions, to be followed by a third. All three project a negative response. No, it is "no good" if someone mouths the words of faith, yet can point to no personal behavior that corresponds with that profession. No, "faith" like that cannot "save" because it is not faith. It amounts to nothing more than meaningless, empty words. Of course, it is of no earthly good to feed a starving man mere words, however sincere, when you could supply a meal. Where are the deeds of mercy that triumph over judgment (2:13)? Simply saying you are a great basketball player, a star reporter, or a true Christian is not good enough. You must demonstrate your skills by an outstanding performance that would convince anyone once they saw it.

In 2:15 the picture of someone "naked" should not be taken literally. Rather, it means that the person has only one undergarment, a floor length tunic, but not two, which was common and necessary for washing. The person also probably does not have a cloak, commonly worn over the tunic, to keep one warm. Perhaps it was stolen or bartered away. This hypothetical person is purposely reminiscent of the "poor person in dirty clothes" who entered the assembly in 2:2. Verse 15 adds the fact that this person is also hungry on a regular basis.

"Lacks daily food" does not mean the person has no food ever, but rather that he does not have enough each day; some food one day, the next no food. In the first century most people made daily wages, usually a denarius coin, which was just enough to get by on. So this person has no job either, or at least no regular work. Also, although "daily food" sounds similar to "Give us this day our daily bread" from the Lord's Prayer (Mt. 6:11), the Greek words are distinctively different.

The phrase "brother or sister" in 2:15 is unique in the New Testament. Modern translations such as NRSV often render the term for "brothers" as "brothers and sisters," but the plural "brothers" does not occur here. Instead, 2:15 employs the two singular words–"brother"and "sister." This suggests that James did not necessarily have in mind only a "Christian" brother or sister as the New Testament normally indicates by the term "brothers" (used that way fifteen times in James). Rather, a fellow human being, whether male or female, is in view. All people are brothers and sisters in our struggle for sustenance in this world into which God has placed us. Helping people with the basic human need to eat and be warm does not depend on what religious stripe they are, only on the true mettle of our own Christian conviction.

It is tempting to view the words of comfort in 2:16 as insincere, perhaps even mean-spirited, seeking simply to get rid of a needy nuisance. Our first glance reading sees Dickens's Scrooge here. Nothing in the context warrants this. Rather, the picture is the opposite, making the point clearer. The words are utterly sincere, but accomplish nothing. Such "comfort" is worthless, even perhaps harmfully dispiriting to a person shivering in cold with a stomach gnawing with hunger pains. The phrase "Go in peace" copies the Hebrew way of bidding farewell (Judg. 18:6; 1 Sam. 20:42; 2 Sam. 15:9). It was commonly employed in the first century and continues today in the contemporary Jewish, "Shalom." The Bible contains no evidence of this greeting being used sarcastically or ironically.

The repetition of "What good is it?" (identical in Greek) at the end of 2:16 (NIV) effectively bookends the opening question of 2:14. The literal meaning is, "What is the gain?" Imagine this second question as emotionally more strident and louder than the first. James has proved his point and now prepares for his "in your face" conclusion. That conclusion (v. 17) is stern and accusing. James pronounced such workless faith to be, in fact, "dead"! This is the thesis of this sermon. It is repeated at the end of each "point" (2:20; 2:26). These concluding words intend to shock and convict you. The Greek word for "dead" refers to a corpse (Lk. 7:15). A corpse isn't even a human being, much less a human being who does not exhibit faith. This pronouncement rings with judgment, as if the listeners are as good as dead spiritually, too—resurrectionless—ripe for God's final condemnation.

Many believers understand the concept of being propelled to do things for God out of their faith commitment. However, James forces us to ask whether we are just keeping "busy" going to meetings and attending church meetings or whether we are investing our service in people all around us who need our help—physical, emotional, or spiritual—whether in or outside the church.

Anyone Can Say They Believe (2:18–20)

To make his second "point," James stages a mini-debate between two antagonists on the value and purpose of works for faith. The first debater proposes that it makes no difference whether you have faith or works because it all comes out the same in the end. One has faith; another has works; so what? Both come across to God and their neighbors as equal. In fact, the first antagonist is satisfied to have either faith or works. In James's scenario, faith goes to the debating opponent while the protagonist receives works. We would expect just the opposite. The debater here may have reasoned that both are gifts from God (see 1 Cor. 12:4–11).

The retort comes immediately, "Show me your faith without your works!" When you play cards, it is impossible to know if someone is bluffing until the player lays the cards out for all to see. So, it is with faith. Whether people have faith or not is immaterial if no one can see it in their lives. Obviously, James was dealing in the purely hypothetical. Surely, everyone who proclaims Christ as Savior has some behavior that corroborates their profession of faith. The point of the first antagonist is that it simply does not matter. Only faith matters. The respondent says it makes all the difference in the world. Real faith includes corresponding behavior. Without this, such faith adds up to zero. There can be no argument about it. Faith and works make up a single fabric of cloth. They are indivisible.

In 2:19 the argument of the second speaker takes one more step, so brilliant it leaves the respondent speechless. Demons, we are reminded, believe in God. Yes, Satan believes in the very one God that Christians and Jews believe in. Yet, all their behavior remains demonic, pitted against God and humanity. So, that doesn't matter? Their belief in God saves them anyway? The absurdity is transparent. The fact that they "shudder" sets them apart from the first antagonist. At least the demons are not deluded into thinking that their belief is all that matters and that their actions have no bearing on their standing before God. They know their works condemn them. So, quite rightly, they fear God and the surety of God's wrath. Their actions are diametrically opposed to their "faith," which makes it absurd to call their belief in God real faith at all. And so it is with people. Behavior that reflects neighbor love is an indivisible aspect of real, saving faith.

The choice of "God is one" as a profession demons share with believers is not a random one in this passage. Like so much of James, it reflects the author's basic Jewish orientation in his thought world because this phrase encompasses the very foundation of Judaism. Monotheism, the belief that God is not divisible or multiple or even irrational, set Judaism and Christianity apart from all other religions of the first century to that point. Romans labeled Christians as "atheists" because they would not profess belief in any gods other than the only one, all-encompassing, true God. This conviction finds its biblical basis in Deuteronomy 6:4: "Hear, O Israel: The LORD our God, the LORD is One" (NIV). This passage forms the opening line of the Shema, the prayer Jews have recited since before the time of Christ. Significantly, the passage in Deuteronomy is completed by the admonition to "love the LORD your God with all your heart, and with all your soul, and with all your might" (6:5). "All your might" presumes intense activity in line with the foundational belief in monotheism.

God's oneness remains foundational in the New Testament (1 Cor. 8:4–6; Gal. 3:20; Eph. 4:6; 1 Tim. 2:5) even as it taught the divinity of Jesus Christ and of the Holy Spirit, leading to the doctrine of the trinity that was developed in the following centuries. Thus, the trinitarian creed confesses belief in three persons in one divine being, not three individual and totally independent beings. For James, the oneness of God should be viewed as a role model of sorts in contrast to the "double-minded" who waver in their trust for God (1:8) and need to repent (4:8). Unity of person implies faithfulness to God and integrity of character. People who are one with themselves will also be one with God and have meaningful prayer lives. They will also be one with Christian brothers and sisters and will contribute to the unity of the Christian community rather than division and strife (4:1–3).

James 2:20 essentially repeats the point of 1:17 and the very clear theme of this section of James: Faith without works is futile. This time, the point is made as a biting rhetorical question posed to the first debating opponent by the second. What stands out is the ridicule of the first debater as "you senseless person"or "you foolish man" (NIV). Only James in the New Testament refers to people with the original Greek word. The word could have been rendered "empty" (Lk. 1:53; Eph. 5:6), "in vain" (1 Cor. 15:10), or even "blockhead" (as Lucy likes to call Charlie

Brown). With this choice language, the rational stupidity of the first debater is placed parallel with the spiritual void of a person who claims to have faith but no works. It is a very clever "cut," or putdown, which comes out of the second opponent's confidence in what he has already shown and in what he will yet prove in his biblical showcase of Abraham, and then Rahab.

The description of the emptiness of faith without works has switched subtly from "dead" in 2:17 to "barren" in 2:20. The Greek word for "barren" artistically plays off of "works" by simply adding a one-letter negative prefix, the Greek letter *alpha.*It is like putting "*un*" in front of "*work*" to get "unwork." The term could apply to a field that has been left fallow, to a person who is lazy (Titus 1:12), a worker who doesn't work (Mt. 20:3; 1 Tim. 5:13) or is ineffective (2 Pet. 1:8), or to a word that is "careless" (Mt. 12:36). Thus, without work, or behavior corresponding to neighbor love that can be observed, faith is "unwork," nothing.

To say we are Christians when we don't do anything Christian is like saying we are golfers when we don't golf, chefs when we don't cook, or parents when we don't parent. It is a false, empty, meaningless claim.

Abraham's Action Shows Faith (2:21–24)

The first of two biblical proof stories focuses on Abraham, the prototype of all who are in a positive, trusting, and saving relationship with God. Through his entire life, Abraham lived out a faith relationship with God. James, however, narrows the lens to focus on the one event that puts everything else about Abraham into perspective: the willingness to sacrifice Isaac at God's command. This was the very son God had promised and then provided through the barren and postmenstrual womb of his wife Sarah. In our logical reasoning God's call for such a cruel act makes absolutely no sense. This is the son of covenant promise. He represented the fulfillment of God's blessings. Through him Abraham would become a great nation. What sense or point could there be in sacrificing Isaac? Yet this made sense and had a point in God's logic and in God's planning. This call for Abraham to sacrifice his son became the ultimate crossroad of Abraham's faith. In similar fashion other seemingly nonsensical expectations God reveals to us may be the touchstones for our developing faith.

The point is that Abraham was willing to believe in God's goodness and God's beneficial will for his life even when he could make no rational sense of it. He was fully prepared to put the knife to his son's throat without reasoning that God would provide an alternate sacrifice of a wandering ram. God looked into the will of Abraham and saw an unswerving trust that had generated the action of hauling Isaac and the wood up the mountain and drawing the knife. The completed act of slaughter was unnecessary.

We should not scrutinize the word *offered* in 2:21 as simply an emotional or mental act Abraham never expected to complete. To God, and certainly to James's point, Abraham's act was just as complete as was God's sacrificial "offering" of his own Son and Jesus "offering" himself as sacrifice (Heb. 7:27; 1 Pet. 2:24). Genesis 22:16–17 speaks of Abraham's offering of Isaac as a completed act: "Because you have done this, and have not withheld your son, your only son, I will indeed bless you, and I will make your offspring as numerous as the stars of heaven and as the sand that is on the seashore."

We tend to think of Abraham as the "ancestor," or "father" of people of Jewish descent. James surprises us a bit by calling Abraham "our father" or "our ancestor," meaning the father of Christians, too. This accents the undeniable Jewish roots of Christianity, but it also underlines the ultimate point of life, responding to God's revelation of God and developing a trusting relationship with God—which Abraham was the first human being to do.

When we get to 2:22, it becomes readily apparent that James did not intend to say that Abraham—or anyone else—is justified by works alone. Rather, acceptance with God occurs when faith and action work together. Neither is sufficient in isolation. The verbs are key here. The first, "was active along with," is an outstanding dynamic translation of a word that refers to people who work alongside each other as coworkers. In fact it is simply the verb "work" with a prefix "co." The second verb, "brought to completion," refers to any action that has been totally accomplished. James's point is that faith is incapable of being fully realized without action. These are not opposites; they are totally synergistic, dependent on each other to be of any value, like two gases such as hydrogen and oxygen require each other to be liquid water.

The quotation in 2:23 sounds like it might be God's concluding pronouncement over Abraham after Abraham's ultimate faith achievement of offering Isaac. In fact, this quotation comes from Genesis 15:6, seven chapters and at least twenty years prior to Genesis 22:17, where Abraham offered Isaac. Thus, the word *fulfilled,* which introduces the quotation of Genesis 15:6, in this respect stands out as correct. A sense of prophetic prediction does occur here and is fulfilled then in Genesis 22. Prior to Genesis 15, Abraham has already done other things that correspond to his trust in God, such as leaving his home in Haran (Gen. 12:4). However, for James and the traditional Jewish understanding, Genesis 15:6 functions as a banner over Abraham's entire life, a journey that reached its peak with his offering of Isaac.

When Paul eyed Genesis 15:6, he saw the word *reckoned* or *credited* (NIV) pop out, and anchored his entire theology of grace on it (Rom. 4). James, however, joins traditional Jewish reflection on Genesis 15:6 and on Abraham's life in seeing the situation more holistically. James focuses on the whole package, not just one word. James looks at how Abraham "believed" and sees evidence of his belief in his actions. He sees that God deemed these actions as setting Abraham apart from every other person up to that point in human history. God accepted Abraham as justified, or righteous, not because Abraham woke up one morning with an emotional, misty-eyed feeling about God, but because of Abraham's lifetime of actions based on a committed relationship to God. This remained true in James's day when Christianity emerged and separated from Judaism. It is still true today.

This becomes crystal clear in James's final note in 2:23. Not only did God accept Abraham as righteous, but James identified Abraham as "the friend of God." We don't usually think of our saving relationship with God as a friendship. Too often we see ourselves as sneaking unscathed through God's condemning judgment because Christ covered our sin through his sacrificial death. Yet friendship is an accurate and helpful way of understanding our relationship with God, especially today when bonding relationships are recognized as critical to a person's well-being. God is personal and wants more than anything a genuine relationship with people. Because the Holy One can and will have nothing to do with evil, our sin prevents a close, deep relationship with our God. Christ's solution does two things. It shows us some of God's personality, and does what is necessary to overcome the obstacle of our sin. Through his death, Jesus makes it possible for us to develop a loving relationship with God through the course of our lives, just as Abraham, our father, did.

It should be noted that no passage in Genesis calls Abraham God's friend. In Isaiah 41:8 and 2 Chronicles 20:7, Abraham is called God's "beloved," which NRSV and others translate as "friend." Clearly, though, James was not searching for a proof text. Rather, he accepted the Jewish tradition of his day, which found *friend* to be the best word to describe God's total acceptance of Abraham into a personal, lifelong relationship.

Those of us more familiar with Paul are startled by the declaration in James 2:24. Doesn't Paul say the opposite: we are not justified by works but by faith alone? Not exactly. Paul does say that "a person is justified by faith apart from works prescribed by the law" (Rom. 3:28) and "those who believe are blessed with Abraham who believed" (Gal. 3:9). He also makes a different application of Genesis 15:9 in Romans 4:3 and Galatians 3:6, emphasizing that Abraham was justified by faith apart from works. However, Paul was most concerned with Jews who were rejecting the gospel of Jesus because they were thinking their obedience to Jewish law was totally sufficient for God to accept them through the divine covenant with Abraham. They failed to see the sinful arrogance of this outlook (Rom. 2) as well as the inherent sin in their lives (Rom. 5) that required a level of sacrifice unachievable apart from the perfect son of God, Jesus Christ.

Paul was just as adamant as James about a person's faith being realized in action corresponding to neighbor love. He emphasizes that a Christian's freedom from the law must be exercised in loving actions toward others (Gal. 5:13; Rom.

12:9–13). Paul was well aware that some could twist his doctrine of grace into a rationalization of sinful liberty (Rom. 6:1, 15). Thus Paul would appreciate what James had to say here. To put it simply, though, Paul was more concerned about the person first entering a relationship with God through Christ. The status of being accepted by God is not in any way something earned through human behavior.

James focuses on people who had previously confessed faith in Christ but were giving up their justified status with God by living their lives as if how they lived made no difference at all to God. They may even have employed selected parts of Paul's teaching to support–in the name of Christ–their sinful lifestyles.

Rahab's Action Shows Faith (2:25–26)

The second proof story reminds the readers of Rahab. A Gentile, a woman, and a prostitute–she would not appear to be a model worthy of emulation. She really represents the total opposite of Abraham in the social spectrum. But maybe that is part of point: The principle of faith and work functioning together can be seen from top to bottom in the scriptural witness. In any case, the principle in many ways is easier to see in the simple story of Rahab. She hid the Hebrew spies who snuck into her city of Jericho. She misled their pursuers, providing the spies with an escape route. She also clearly professed her faith in God, telling the spies, "The LORD your God is indeed God in heaven above and on earth below" (Josh. 2:11). Eventually she married Salmon, an Israelite who became an ancestor of King David and of Jesus Christ (Mt. 1:5).

James 2:26 sums up the principle being proved in this section, stating it a third and final time. This time an analogy is added to the description of actionless faith as "dead." A lifeless body, a corpse, is an apt analogy. Since a corpse does not move, perform any action, or even breathe ("without the spirit"), it is presumed to be dead, even today (modern medical devices not withstanding). James wants us to ask, What conclusions can we draw from this? What is God's attitude toward people whose behavior does not reflect neighbor love or any of the other principles of Jesus' teaching? The clear answer appears to be: they are not followers of Jesus; they don't believe in

Christ. Indeed, people without Abraham's and Rahab's faith and works are not Christians; they have no faith, no saving relationship. Whatever they say they believe, their actions prove otherwise.

Sermon

Show Me Your Faith

(James 2:14-26)

If James ministered in the United States today, he might want to preach in the state of Missouri, the "show me" state. James views the Christian life through the window of practical theology: "Don't just tell me you believe; show me."

The need for both faith and works is more clearly seen in this passage than any other New Testament letter. Remember, James addressed Christians, people who had professed faith in Jesus as Savior and Lord. This has everything to do with deeds that demonstrate our faith, not deeds that seek to merit God's grace. This balance between faith and deeds is not to be taken lightly; it strikes at the heart of commitment. In the context of this chapter, James demanded, "Don't just tell me about your commitment to Christ; let me see it in the way you live."

In our health-conscious culture, everything is going "lite." Product A has 60 percent less fat than it used to have; product B has 40 percent fewer calories than its competition. Everything we eat is changing. My Grandfather Ellsworth started a dairy business in the 1920s. He bought milk from the farmers, homogenized it, pasteurized it, and bottled it for retail sale. In the early days the dairy could not market two percent milk. They often gave it to the farmers to feed the hogs. They called the rich, "half and half" milk and cream mixture, "cereal milk." Ordinary whole milk was not considered creamy enough for cereal. How times have changed! Not only is two percent milk marketable today, our daughters think it is too rich! Now one percent or skim milk seems to be the preferred choice of the health-conscious. "Lite" is right! *Leadership Magazine* published a cartoon of a church that sought to draw a crowd with a promise contained in these words on the marquee sign:

24% fewer commitments
Home of the 7.5% tithe
Sermons—only 15 minutes long
45 minute worship services
We have only 8 commandments—your choice
We use only 3 spiritual laws and Cliff's notes for our
    Scripture text
Everything you've ever wanted in a church...and less![1]

What may be healthy for one's eating habits is not necessarily positive in other areas. When it comes to spiritual matters, James isn't into "lite" anything! He challenges Christians to rise to the top, like fresh cream. When it comes to demonstrating one's faith, James offers no choices—it is all or nothing.

Concerned for the lack of action he saw in the church, James explored some areas of Christian living that were (and are) just too lite for his taste!

Words Are Not Enough (2:14–17)

James was a great illustrator of biblical truth. He created word pictures that any child can understand. Here's the first snapshot: It is a Sunday morning. You hurriedly take your place in the pew as the prelude winds down and the service is about to start. While you are catching your breath, you glance at the person next to you. Surprisingly, you do not recognize your pew partner. He is poorly dressed at best. A lingering glance suggests that he has not eaten well for some time. Your heart is touched with your "pewmate's" condition, and you softly pray, "Lord, I am so thankful that you have blessed me so that I'm not in this condition." As communion is passed, the person next to you humbly partakes. He must be a brother in the Lord, you conclude. Now your heart is moved even more. When the last "Amen" is uttered, you quickly step over and, with moist eyes, shake his hand firmly, offering these thoughtful words, "Brother, I wish you the best: Stay warm and eat well. I'm so glad you were here today." You turn and walk out of the worship center feeling the warm glow of Christian compassion.

Common sense should dictate that this is a ridiculous response. There is a time for heartfelt prayer and encouraging words, but there is also a time for action. The story is told of a frontier congregation. They had gathered at the church building to pray for a family whose log home had been destroyed by a twister on the prairie. One pioneer mother and her children arrived a little late. As they took their place in the little church building, one of the older, pious members smugly asked, "Isn't your husband coming?" She responded softly, "No, he can't come this evening, but he sent his prayers in the wagon." Outside was a wagon bed full of food and supplies.

I am not suggesting that prayer isn't relevant. I am insisting that the Bible says God expects us to act as we pray. One is not more important than the other, but a combination of the two makes for a powerful Christian testimony. James rightly concluded that faith not accompanied by deeds is a dead or useless faith, both outwardly and inwardly.

"*Dead*" here is the word for "corpse." Without deeds that give credence to faith, a person is as good as dead spiritually. Words are cheap; actions always speak louder. James would have nothing to do with such a "lite" faith! A faith that responds in action is the result of a personal relationship with Jesus Christ. To be sure, not everyone who knows Jesus Christ is compassionate, thoughtful, and selfless, but without Christ, true compassion may not be possible.

Jean Rousseau was a French deist philosopher and author of the 1700s. Describing him, R. Kent Hughes writes:

> Rousseau was the first intellectual to repeatedly proclaim himself the friend of all mankind. He said he was a man born to love and in fact taught the doctrine of love more persistently than many preachers of the day. How did he actually relate to humanity? His father though ill-tempered meant nothing to him but an inheritance. His only concern for his long-lost brother was to certify him dead so he could get the family money. All five of his children were unnamed and were placed immediately after birth in a hospital for infants

where two thirds of all babies died in the first year. None of his children survived. Rousseau, the self-proclaimed lover of humanity, did not even record the dates of his children's births.[2]

Words and Titles Are Cheap!

Preacher and author Elton Trueblood said, "Our faith becomes practical when it is expressed in two books: the date book and the checkbook."[3] Words are simply not enough. Without supporting deeds, good words point to a "lite" faith.

Belief Is Not Enough (2:18–20)

Sometimes we delude ourselves into believing that the ability to do good is a gift that God gives to some and not to others. Someone might respond, "Okay, you've got deeds, I've got faith. Both of us are valuable in the kingdom, right?" Actions are not optional; deeds are not for extra credit; good works are not bonus points on the test of faith. One without the other is insufficient for all Christians.

Jesus used the example of a tree and its fruit to warn about false teachers whose words are not backed up by genuine deeds. A good tree, he said, produces good fruit, and a bad tree, bad fruit. Every tree that does not produce good fruit is cut down and destroyed (Mt. 7:15–19). That makes logical sense, horticulturally speaking. Then Jesus spelled out the analogy. "Thus you will know them by their fruits" (Mt. 7:20). You may not qualify as a false teacher, but the analogy holds true: You will be known by your fruit! Jesus' point is simple: Good faith is always accompanied by good deeds.

In case the reader remains unconvinced, James landed the knockout punch with his next statement: "You are proud of the fact that you believe; let me tell you, you are in good company. Even the demons believe, and they tremble" (2:19, author's paraphrase). A contemporary proverb teaches that during war there are no atheists in the foxholes. In spiritual war there are no atheists among the enemy. All the demonic forces believe and shudder. They are scared to death because their works have condemned them.

The irony of this seems to be lost on most of us. We fear demons but have lost our fear of God. Maybe that is the result of an imbalanced emphasis between the grace of God and the wrath of God. We are more comfortable with the picture of the Lamb of God than the Lion of Judah. Donald McCullough writes, "When the true story gets told, whether in the partial light of historical perspective or in the perfect light of eternity, it may well be revealed that the worst sin of the church at the end of the twentieth century has been the trivialization of God."[4] Take a lesson from the demons: There is no room for "lite" faith in this spiritual foxhole.

This distinction needs to be made. Simply believing God exists is not the equivalent of true faith. Beliefs must lead to implicit trust. Such trust must then respond with action before it can be called true faith. For instance, you may believe the parachute will save you if the plane is going down, but this is not faith until you trust the chute enough to jump out into thin air. You may believe the surgeon can heal you, but this is not faith until you trust the surgeon enough to lie down on the operating table and start counting backwards. You may believe your true love's proposal for marriage, but it is not faith until you trust your beloved enough to walk down the aisle and say, "I do." Hebrews 11 is known as the faith chapter of the Bible. Listen to how each person in this hall of faith is described: Abel offered; Enoch pleased; Noah built; Abraham looked; Isaac blessed; Jacob worshiped; Joseph instructed; Moses chose; the Israelites passed through; Rahab welcomed; and the list goes on. Each person's faith is described in action words!

Consider an ordinary tree. The leaves of that tree use up precious nutrients in the process of photosynthesis, but as the leaves consume the nutrients in the sap, a suction is formed that draws more sap from the roots. Without the sap, the leaves and branches would die. The continual flow of this sap comes only as it is used up by the leaves. So it is with faith and deeds. Through our faith we draw life from Christ, but a continual supply of fresh spiritual nutrients depends on our willingness to "consume" or use up those spiritual nutrients through deeds or acts of obedience.

Once again, James returned to his theme in these verses with a little different twist. Instead of the word *dead* or *corpse*, he used the phrase "faith apart from works is barren" (2:20). This paints a vivid picture. *Barren* creates the image of a womb that produces no life.

Jesus warned his followers that deeds, not words, tell the true story.

> "Not everyone who says to me, 'Lord, Lord,' will enter the kingdom of heaven, but only the one who does the will of my Father in heaven. On that day many will say to me, 'Lord, Lord, did we not prophesy in your name, and cast out demons in your name, and do many deeds of power in your name?' Then I will declare to them, 'I never knew you; go away from me, you evildoers.'" (Mt. 7:21–23)

Goodness Is Not Enough (2:21–26)

Sometimes we conclude that if we are good enough God will be pleased to take us to heaven. Someone might say wistfully, "I hope I die on a good day, when I've done more good than bad so the scales of heaven will balance in my favor." This misses the point totally; one's goodness is not the issue.

Some Bible scholars argue that James 2:23 stands in conflict with Paul's teaching of justification by faith. Such an interpretation ignores the perspective from which each of the biblical authors write. Paul taught that we are justified—set right with God—by faith; James said by deeds. Who then is right? Both! Paul spoke of being justified before God only; James was concerned about being justified before both God and humanity. Paul is preconversion; James is postconversion. Paul is talking about a faith that saves; James is talking about a faith that obeys. Both are right, and each is important. We are not good enough, but God is!

God's Grace Is Enough (2:21–26)

James uses two Old Testament examples to make his point about God's grace. The first is Abraham. Abraham trusted God, and God's grace was enough for him. Everything that Abraham did was an expression of faith: He followed God's lead to a new place; he waited twenty-five years to have a son according to God's promise; he willingly offered that son as a sacrifice at God's command, believing that God would raise him from the dead. "You see that his faith and his actions were working together, and his faith was made complete by what he did" (Jas. 2:22, NIV). As a result, God called Abraham "his friend" (2:23). That is grace, and it is enough. More importantly, you and I can say that we are friends of Jesus. How can we be sure of that? Jesus assures us: "You are my friends if you do what I command you" (Jn. 15:14).

The second Old Testament example is Rahab (Josh. 2). She was a pagan prostitute living in the city of Jericho when the Israelites began their conquest of the Promised Land. Though not of the Hebrew race, she was of the household of faith. Her deeds tell the story of her faith. When the city of Jericho was destroyed, God saved her and her family. But that is not all. She later married a Hebrew man and became a part of the lineage of Jesus Christ (Mt. 1:5). That is grace, and it is enough.

One more time, James returned to his theme for this passage: "Faith without deeds is dead" (2:26, NIV). James would have no part of a "lite" faith. Neither should we!

CHAPTER 5

Respecting the Danger of the Tongue
JAMES 3:1–12

Exegesis

James appears to set off on a totally new course with chapter three, making a clear-cut shift from 2:14–26. We must remember, however, that James includes speech as a prime area of a person's works. So this new section is not that far from the faith and works theme of 2:14–26. A person's speech reveals discrimination of others (2:1–4) and lack of neighbor love every bit as much as does a physical act (2:12).

Chapter three is a planned expansion on being "slow to speak" from the thematic proverb of 1:19 and the brief touch in 1:26. Its relationship to hearing God ("quick to listen") may not be immediately obvious. Our inability to control our harmful speech functions as a reliable indicator of our inability to hear God speak God's will and wisdom to us in a way that it can improve our lives. This is a balancing act in a certain respect, because our speech is so powerfully evil that none of us have the spiritual capacity to subdue it fully.

The Impossibility of Controlling Our Speech (3:1–2)

James frames his exposition on controlling our speech with the responsibility of being a teacher in the church. But James did not follow up on this after 3:1. This suggests that his primary concern was, in fact, our speech. Teaching functions more as an example or illustration to apply to concrete life situations the vital responsibility we all have to control our speech.

Teaching normally involves a great deal of talking, whether in lecture or at the personal, tutorial level. Thus its capacity to harm fellow believers in their relationship to God and to others is profound. It is not just the moments of teaching per se that are at issue; it is also the moral example set by a teacher's everyday interaction with people. A teacher is one of the most admired members of a community, Christian or otherwise. People far beyond the student body watch and observe the teacher's personal behavior, especially the teacher's manner and content in talking.

Like rabbis in Judaism, teachers in the early church were highly valued and respected. At the local level, teachers appear to have functioned as one of the primary leaders in the early church (Acts 13:1; Rom. 12:7; 1 Cor. 12:28; Eph. 4:11). Perhaps only the apostles, who functioned more as traveling outside authorities, carried more prestige in matters of doctrine and ethical teaching. How this related to the appointed office of elder is unsure. Elders were expected to be "apt to teach." It would appear that some elders were teachers, but that not all teachers were necessarily elders, since being an elder included additional qualifications (1 Tim. 3:1–7; Titus 1:5–9). Regardless, a teacher's primary job was to transmit the teachings of the apostles accurately and apply them faithfully to the local church (2 Tim. 2:2). Is this comparable to the contemporary "minister"? Probably, but also to all teachers in the church, from those who lead small group Bible studies to those who instruct first-graders at vacation Bible school.

James intends for teachers to take his warning very seriously. Being a teacher is not a perk that earns special favors from God. Remember, God does not show favoritism. In fact, James emphasizes that God will apply even stricter judgment to a person with so much responsibility in the church. So, James seeks to take the wind out of the sails of aspiring, but not yet ready or qualified, believers who desired to teach. Why were such people disqualified as teachers? It may have been a matter of maturity or knowledge. It may also have included their personal, spiritual, and moral qualities, especially their speech.

James includes himself as a teacher. As such he presents himself as one willing to bear the mantle of responsibility that he is talking about. He stood ready to receive God's careful scrutiny even as he understood the risks involved. This notion of stricter assessment of teachers may have depended on knowledge of Jesus' teaching: "From the one to whom much has been entrusted, even more will be demanded" (Lk. 12:48b). James may have known Jesus' pronouncement against Jewish teachers of the law who abused their responsibility to widows. Jesus said, "they will receive the greater condemnation" (Mk. 12:40).

James 3:2 introduces the thesis statement demonstrated in the exposition that continues through 3:12. The logic of the verse is simple: Since people cannot achieve moral perfection, they cannot attain absolute control of their speech. The tone throughout is negative and disheartening. Even facing a fight we cannot win, we have to do the best we can to control our tongues, which are so powerful, destructive, and evil.

Throughout, James personifies our "tongue" to capture the seeming independence of our talk from our will. In reading his remarks, we have to keep reminding ourselves that it is indeed our talk, our personal, everyday speech he is depicting as so evil and so irresistible to our efforts to manage it. To dig deeper spiritually, what James depicts is really the everyday battles between our own two wills, our evil versus our good will, or the part of ourselves to which we continue to provide Satan free access versus that part we have surrendered to God through Christ. To put it bluntly, despite the desire for improvement in the way we talk to one another, our good will never wins all the battles and never will.

The Greek word translated as "make many mistakes" more literally means to "stumble," as when our foot strikes an impediment and causes us to fall. New Testament writers commonly employ it as a euphemism for sin (Rom. 11:11; 2 Pet. 1:10, and already in Jas. 2:10 [NIV]). It describes our encounter with a situation in life that, for whatever reasons, leads us to choose against God's will and thus fail. It is not a blunder for which we are not held accountable; it is sin for which God holds us very accountable. So James reminds us that the ways in which we sin are beyond enumerating. He notes specifically that our sins of speech fall under this rubric also, in many and variegated ways.

James theorizes that if we could somehow stop the flood of sinful speech that flows from our mouths, this would stop up all our other kinds of sin, too. This is not to say that we only commit sins of speech, so stopping them stops all sin. Rather, it says that since speech sins are the most difficult to stop, if we could stop them, then we surely could stop all the rest. However, the sad reality is that we can't ever accomplish either feat because this could only be done if we were perfect, which we are most patently not.

The Powerful Evil of Our Speech (3:3–6)

James uses three analogies to enhance our understanding of the tongue's disastrous capabilities. Despite its relatively small size, the tongue is capable of overpowering the rest of our body and leading us to devastate the lives of others around us. The first two analogies begin innocently enough. They simply provide examples of small things, that, when controlled, determine the movement of large things–bits in horses mouths, rudders on ships. However, the last analogy–fire–adds powerful imagery to the destructive capabilities of the tongue. James expands this into the controlling image of the tongue.

Repetition of the bridle imagery connects James 3:3 to 3:2. Although the NRSV speaks of "bridle" in 3:2 and "bit" in 3:3, it is the same Greek word in both places. Essentially a bit is part of a bridle and is the more focused image. It goes into the horse's mouth, presses against its tongue, and makes it possible to control the horse's movements by a tug on the reins. Also repeated in both 3:2 and 3:3 is the phrase, "the whole body." The idea for both humans and horses is that you can guide the whole if you control the key bodily focal point, the tongue. The horse is a great illustration of the point. Modern illustrations expand this universal truth: power buttons on electronic equipment, computer chips, ignition keys, and steering wheels on cars and machines.

The rudder and ship analogy draws on a rudder's similarity to a tongue and enlarges the proportional distinction between the small thing and the thing it directs. It also widens the analogy to include the challenge of dealing with unpredictable, powerful outside forces. The rudder, if guided by an expert, can harness not just the ship, but the winds and the waves as well, keeping the ship on course and even speeding it on to the destination.

Our lives, like life on the open sea, are pounded daily by outside forces that can have positive or negative impact on our speech. Failure to adapt these forces in a positive way will inevitably lead to loss of direction, perhaps even to destruction on the rocks (compare 1:6–7). The repetition in verses 3 and 4 of the Greek word translated as "guide" and "directs" allows some hope that our speech can be influenced for good if it is controlled and guided properly. James, however, does not explore further the positive potential of this image. Instead, vulnerability to bad influences by outside forces crowns the picture of this analogy in 3:5–6.

Verse 5 specifies the point of the horse and ship analogies. Locking onto the proportional smallness of the "tongue" in humans, horses, and ships is expected. However, emphasizing their activity of great "boasts" surprises us. We can understand a person boasting, but not a horse or a ship. This negative personification of the tongue, it seems, has more to do with where James is headed next, to the evil of the tongue, than to what is present in the first two analogies.

James's teaching about the tongue resonates with a classical Greek moral story. The Greek tale depicts the tongue arguing with the other members of the body about who is the greatest. The arms, legs, hands, and head heap abuse on the tongue as the least important because it is so small. The tongue swears an oath to the others that before the day is over, they will all acknowledge its superiority. As circumstances would have it, the king just happens to be passing by, and the tongue causes the person of whom it was a part to utter an obscenity at him. As this offending man is about to be executed later that day, the tongue demands that all the other parts of the body pay homage to its importance. When they do, the tongue offers an apology to the king, causing the man to be released.

James offers a raging forest fire as imagery fitting for the destructive capacities of a boasting tongue, or for any tongue that is out of control, unguided. One small boast, insult, retort, or falsehood can destroy a person's life or the lives of families, communities, countries, even the world. Devastating wars have begun in such ways. Closer to home for most of us, just a few words can rampage through relationships of all kinds. To expand on the image a little, intentionality does not lessen the resulting damage of a spark or a word. The destruction is the same even if the spark is accidental or the word careless. The fire analogy draws attention to the importance of controlling our speech as best we can, just like we need to be careful with matches.

Rather than telling us how we should go about controlling our speech and thus limiting its destructiveness, James 3:6 expands on how, like a fire, the human tongue is so incorrigibly evil. After baldly calling the tongue "fire," James unpacks the tongue's evil in four clauses, each describing a different dimension of its evil.

The first clause brands the tongue as the focal point for evil in the human body. "Iniquity" is simply the negation of the word *righteous* in Greek. "World" in the New Testament normally refers to the sinful, ungodly pattern of human behavior to be avoided. That interpretation would only duplicate "iniquity" here. It can also refer to the mode or organization by which something is accomplished. Adopting this understanding, we see James calling our tongues the primary vehicles or perhaps the chief executive officers of our unrighteousness. The tongue outranks any other parts of our body, or "members." "Is placed," with the passive indicating a divine subject, implies that this *in charge* function of the human tongue is simply the way God designed human beings. In creating the capacity for speech, God allowed our speech to be a fount from which our sinful condition can flow.

The second dimension of the tongue's evil is that its corruption affects all the other parts of our body, our entire person in every respect. The Greek word translated here as "stains" refers to making something dirty or defiled. It appears in the New Testament only here and at Jude 23. Think of the tongue producing a dye that you continually swallow. The digestion process disseminates the dye to all the organs, bones, and tissues of the body. Eventually, the entire body changes color, becomes "stained" from the inside out. The condition has no remedy; it is permanent. In this sense, the sinful things we say contaminate our whole being. Our sins of speech continuously and consistently illuminate our "sinful nature," to use a phrase more familiar to Paul's theology of sin. James is unique in picturing the tongue as the center of this sinful nature.

The third dimension of the tongue's evil moves beyond the borders of human bodies or individuals. It depicts the damage the tongue inflicts on human society at large. The way this is stated may sound a bit odd to us. However, "the cycle of nature," or literally, "wheel of birth" (NRSV alt.) was extremely common terminology among Greek philosophers. It represented what we might call in the Shakespearian sense, "fate." It refers to those forces outside oneself that determine or at least impact our lives. The ancient world deemed it impossible for people somehow to operate outside their "wheel of birth." So James teaches us that this very pattern of human existence–the social dynamics of life, the very sphere of existence in which we all operate–has been and continues to be corrupted by the destructiveness of our speech. It is aflame in the process of destruction. In other words, my harmful speech does not affect only myself but everyone around me and everyone around them and so on and so on. In like manner, everyone else's harmful speech, past and present, damages me. We have no way out of its devastation.

The fourth dimension of the tongue's evil names the source of its evil. We cannot blame God, who created us with the capacity for speech and for sin. Rather, the entire blame falls on the one who originated sin and evil–Satan. James did not use the word *Satan*, but rather a euphemism for him, *hell*. It is important to make clear the distinction between "hell" and "Hades" in the New Testament. "Hades," in the Jewish conception of afterlife, is where people go when they die (Mt. 11:23; 16:18; Lk. 10:15; 16:23; Acts 2:27, 31; Rev. 1:18; 6:8; 20:13–14). It is a morally and spiritually neutral term. "Hell" (*Gehenna*), found here, is the place of everlasting punishment (Mt. 5:22, 29–30; 10:28; 18:9; 23:15, 33; Mk. 9:43–47; Lk. 12:5; Jas. 3:6).

Some evidence indicates that in New Testament times *Gehenna* referred to a constantly smoldering garbage dump outside the walls of Jerusalem. Much earlier, it was a valley south of Jerusalem once used for pagan fire sacrifices, an appropriate way of depicting God's punishment on Israel for betraying God (2 Kings 23:10; 2 Chr. 28:3; 33:6; Jer. 7:31; 32:35). The association with "fire" and destruction makes it a most fitting way for James to connect Satan's evil designs with the inroads the tongue, or human speech, provides. The tongue, in the end, is the agent or tool of Satan. This explains why its effects are so devastating and why it is so impossible for us to keep it under control.

The Resistant Will of Evil Speech (3:7–8)

Having described the utter evil and destructiveness of the tongue, James next draws attention to an irony of creation–the human ability to subdue every other animal of creation, often using our speech to do so, contrasted with our complete inability to subdue our tongues. This ironic observation reinforces the negative tone we have seen throughout the discussion: The best we can do is to moderate our evil speech; we cannot eliminate it.

The Greek word translated here as "species" normally refers to things of nature (Rom. 1:26; 2:14, 27; 11:21, 24; 1 Cor. 11:14; Gal. 2:15; 4:8; Eph. 2:3; Jas. 3:7; 2 Pet. 1:4). Although the modern, scientific concept of "species" was not known in the first century, the basic differences among animals certainly were. James probably depends on Genesis 1:26, 28. His categories, except for reptile, line up with the creatures named there, and certainly his concept of human domination over other creatures is grounded in this passage. Outside this chapter, the Greek word for "tamed" appears only in Mark 5:4, where it is translated "subdue." It should not be narrowed to the way we "tame" our house pets. In that case, the point James makes is untrue. We haven't made house pets of tigers and crocodiles or any number of creatures. However, humans do dominate or subdue all other creatures. Through hunting, fishing, and other means, we capture them, cage them, and kill them, as well as "tame" them.

In drawing the conclusion that we are unable to "tame" our tongues, James cleverly depicts the human tongue as a deadly, poisonous snake. This is such an apt picture because of how our tongues, like serpents, can strike out so quickly to do their damage. It is also apt because of how a serpent was Satan's vehicle for cleverly deceiving Eve to sin against God (Gen. 3:1–6). James was not the first to draw this comparison between poisonous snakes and the evil of the human tongue. The connection is made also in Psalms 58:4; 140:3; and Job 20:12–16. Job interestingly pictures the poison being swallowed internally and ultimately ending the life of the person doing the poisoning.

The Consistent Evil of Our Speech (3:9–12)

We must read 3:9 in light of the analogies in 3:11–12. Then we will see the central point: Our tongues are naturally evil, and this is a reality of creation that cannot be changed. We have to learn to live with this evil albatross around our necks. This doesn't mean that we cannot or should not make moral and spiritual inroads against this evil. At the same time we must come to grips with the stark reality that we will never win a complete victory. We can never let down our guard. We will always have to contend with the evil of our tongues, personally and socially.

James 3:9 points to another irony of life, that both good and evil come from our mouths. This is the only time in this whole discussion that anything good about the tongue has been acknowledged. The point is illustrated by epitomizing the best and the worst use of human speech—praising God and cursing other people. Other utterances in a spectrum of best to worst could have been offered. However, for James this contrast is incomparably ironic. Calling people "those who are made in the likeness of God" makes the point that in cursing the highest creation of God we are ultimately cursing God. It is the ultimate in hypocrisy to praise God through worship and prayer at one moment, only in the next to curse out a fellow human. Such behavior calls into question the veracity of our worship and the genuineness of our devotion to God.

James censures this sorry state of affairs in 3:10. "This ought not to be" challenges us to improve, but it offers no permanent solution. It calls us to fight this tendency to continue to allow our tongues to rule our lives, but we have to keep in mind that James believes no overturn of human nature is possible, only improved control. This becomes crystal clear in the illustrations offered in 3:11–12. Human nature, with regard to the dominating evil of our speech, cannot be changed any more than a tiger can change its stripes or an elephant shorten its trunk.

James makes his point with water springs and fruit-bearing plants. Using questions helps draw us into the realistic view of ourselves that James desired. Of course, a spring cannot alternate between fresh water and salt water. Of course, a fig tree cannot just decide to change its nature so that it can produce olives. A grapevine can never bear figs. They are the way they are because God made them that way. The situation is the same with our tongues. God has created us with the ability to speak freely. This always and forever has become a channel for our natural evil to spew out to harm all those around us. We must control this natural reality, but we cannot change it.

The Greek word translated here as "fresh" literally means "sweet" (Jas. 3:11–12; Rev. 10:9–10) and comes into English as *glucose*. What is in mind is the fabulous "sweet" taste of great spring water. This is contrasted with "brackish," a word appearing only in this chapter in the New Testament. The meaning is not necessarily salty, but just bitter or bad tasting, a sharp contrast to sweet-tasting water. James denies the possibility of such salty, bitter water changing into sweet, fresh water. Thus he identifies the human mouth as a spring with bad-tasting water. Our capacity for human speech brings harm and hurt, and this will never be reversed!

SERMON

Tongue in Check

(James 3:1–12)

This text troubles me! James issued a warning for us who teach in the church: "For you know that we who teach will be judged with greater strictness." Does this mean that we who teach and preach will be held to a higher standard? Or did James mean we "will be punished more severely"?

What is it about teaching that is so dangerous for a Christian? The teacher may find it difficult to maintain a proper sense of humility. Teaching provides you with more frequent opportunities to put your foot in your mouth, where it does not belong. Teaching provides an avenue to promote one's own agenda, not God's. A teacher is responsible for what he or she teaches, for it will lead other people closer to or farther away from God. James will not let the teacher claim ignorance. Jesus gave the same warning. Listen to this parable from Luke 12:47–48:

> "That slave who knew what his master wanted, but did not prepare himself or do what was wanted, will receive a severe beating. But the one who did not know and did what deserved a beating will receive a light beating. From everyone to whom much has been given, much will be required; and from the one to whom much has been entrusted, even more will be demanded."

If that isn't scary enough, listen to these words from Matthew 12:36–37: "I tell you, on the day of judgment you will have to give an account for every careless word you utter; for by your words you will be justified, and by your words you will be condemned."

James moved from this specific warning for teachers to a general warning about the dangers of the tongue. No simple activity carries more potential danger than talking, and no member of the human body can mess up a day faster than the tongue. The damage created by a one-minute verbal tirade may take hours, days, or even years to repair. Not one of us is perfect when it comes to use of the tongue. If talking were the only way we could possibly sin, we would all still be guilty! James did not cut us any slack in chapter three. He put God's truth where our mouths are. The Bible both warns and instructs us in the matter of godly speech. This is not an easy lesson. This is radical oral surgery without anesthetic!

Beware the Controlling Tongue (3:3–5)

James illustrates the tongue's power by noting the controlling power of three other objects: a bit in a horse's mouth, the rudder on a ship, and a spark that ignites a forest fire. In each case the controlling object is much smaller than what is being controlled. Such is the power of the tongue. Though small, it controls how the world perceives us. This warning label was found on a fountain pen some years ago: "When this pen runs too freely, it is nearly empty." I think we could borrow that wisdom and apply it to this very passage: "When this tongue runs too freely, the brain is nearly empty." Nothing indicates a weak mind more than an overly active tongue. God designed us so that what we think would control what we say. Unfortunately, most of us are guilty of saying things we haven't thought of yet. Do not let the tongue's diminutive size fool you. It is small but potentially destructive.

In September, 1995, a squirrel climbed onto the Metro-North Railroad power lines near New York City. This set off an electrical surge, which weakened an overhead bracket, which let a wire dangle toward the tracks, which tangled in a train, which tore down all the lines. As a result, 47,000 commuters were stuck in Manhattan for hours that evening.[1]

All of this damage resulted from one small squirrel. As bad as that mass transit nightmare was, it cannot hold a candle to the damage the little tongue has done and continues to do.

Beware the Consuming Tongue (3:6)

James's second warning is that the tongue itself is a fire. Now, a fire that is under control is a very useful power, but out of control the fire becomes devastating. Stately forests that have taken several lifetimes to mature can be reduced to ashes in a few hours or days. The comparisons of fire with the tongue can easily be multiplied.

Fire creates heat. We refer to heated arguments and fiery language. When someone is exploding verbally, we say that the person is hot under the collar. "What he or she said really burned me." The analogy of James is a fitting one. The tongue really is a fire.

Fire destroys property. I will never forget the sight, sounds, and smell of the fire that destroyed the Sherwood Oaks Christian Church building in the fall of 1991. I stood watching helplessly as the blaze consumed a building that for me felt like a second home. The sinister-looking flames took great delight in towering over me and destroying my office. What destruction! When the fire was finally extinguished, what remained looked like an aerial bomb destruction we see in photos from World War II! I managed to retrieve some items that were in my office at the time. To this day they retain the acrid odor of that black, billowing smoke.

In similar fashion, I've seen fiery words destroy careers, marriages, parent/child relationships, friendships, self-esteem, confidence, hope, and the desire to keep on living. That is just the short list. Whoever penned the sentiment, "Sticks and stones may break my bones, but words will never hurt me," didn't have a clue. Words do hurt, and we use them far too often as a tool to destroy.

Fire leaves scars. The congregation went through a relocation following the fire. Still, every time I pass the old location and see the exposed concrete foundations where the building once stood, I remember the wee hours of that destructive September morning. Not a week goes by that I do not pick up a book in my study and find that it has crinkled pages from the smoke and water damage of those few hours. Those scars will be there for as long as I keep those books. It is easy to forget that the words spoken in heated arguments will leave scars long after the passions have cooled. James is right; the tongue is a fire! Keep it under control, and it will bring warmth and joy to your relationships, like a cozy fireplace on a winter's night. Let it loose, and it will become a raging inferno, consuming you and all whom you love.

James 3:6 powerfully describes the hideous nature of the tongue in four clauses. Each clause reflects a different facet of the tongue's potential evil. First, it is "a world of iniquity" or "evil" (NIV). It stands in contrast to everything righteous. Second, it "stains the whole body." What flows from the tongue permeates mind, heart, soul, and will so that an individual's character is colored or stained by the tongue's poison. Third, it "sets on fire the cycle of nature" or "the course of life" (NIV). The social dynamic of the culture in which we live is controlled and corrupted by the tongue. Fourth, James points us to the source of the tongue's fiery nature–hell itself. The word used here is *Gehenna*, the name that referred to the refuse dump outside of Jerusalem where the fires burned continually. What a fitting description for the smoldering garbage that often comes from the tongue!

Beware the Contrary Tongue (3:7–8)

The third warning involves the contrary nature of the tongue. To illustrate this negative power, James turned to the untamed nature of wild animals. While nearly every animal can be tamed, the tongue remains untamable. "To tame" means to bring about a change in something or someone that will render it useful or beneficial.

Trained animals have always fascinated me. Our daughters, Emily and Rebekah, worked hard at teaching tricks to our dog, Toby. He will sit, jump up, and shake hands, all for the anticipation of a doggy treat. Here is the picture that James painted: The trainer in the lion's cage is in less danger from the king of the beasts than from the wimpiest person who unleashes the tongue. Only by the grace of God and the presence of the Holy Spirit can one keep the tongue at bay.

Beware the Condemning Tongue (3:9–12)

James's last example concerns inconsistent condemnation. Have you ever wondered what it would be like if you had to verbalize everything you were thinking? What if you could not soften the bluntness of your thoughts and had to say what you really felt about that new hairdo, decorating scheme, or job promotion? That would be awful; yet we are often guilty of much worse. How can a Christian praise God on Sunday morning and then on Monday verbally beat up on those around him? Some do not even wait until Monday. I can read the lips of those leaving the church parking lot after services! One does not sip both fresh water and salt water from the same drinking fountain. One does not harvest olives from a fig tree or figs from a grape vine. So how do we justify the contrasting speech of praise and condemnation?

This may well be the most convicting paragraph yet. Some wise sage said, "The tongue is the only instrument that grows sharper with use." I fear that the church has made gossip the Christian's acceptable sin. We have been told, "You can't believe everything you hear," but no one ever said we couldn't repeat it. Have you noticed that gossip always seems to travel fastest over grapevines that are slightly sour? Gossip is like mud thrown on a clean wall. It may not stick, but it always leaves a dirty mark. We have all but forgotten the very important biblical principle that would stem 90 percent of all gossip. If you have problems with or have been hurt by another individual, go to that individual first and work it out. Telling someone else about the problem instead of the person who has offended you only hurts; it never heals. Once you have shared that story with another person, no matter how credible, the story is no longer within your control.

World War II produced the expression, "Loose lips sink ships." In other words, do not utter a word about what you may know regarding the war effort; it might be overheard by the wrong ears and endanger the lives those who are fighting for freedom. Loose lips don't sink just ships. They sink marriages, relationships, friendships, and reputations. You and I have a moral and scriptural obligation to work through our issues without gossip.

Read again these words of Jesus in Matthew 18:15–17:

> "If another member of the church sins against you, go and point out the fault when the two of you are alone. If the member listens to you, you have regained that one. But if you are not listened to, take one or two others along with you, so that every word may be confirmed by the evidence of two or three witnesses. If the member refuses to listen to them, tell it to the church; and if the offender refuses to listen even to the church, let such a one be to you as a Gentile and a tax collector."

That is difficult advice to practice. It is so much easier to cry on another's shoulder, sharing your hurts and disappointments, than it is to work through the problem with the offending party. However, it is important to keep in mind that our emotions can paint a distorted picture of the truth. I have often seen a potential disaster averted by a mature Christian who made sure he or she had all the facts before reacting. Untold hurt and lasting damage have been avoided.

When a friend comes to you with a juicy tidbit of gossip, ask, "Have you talked with your offender yet? If not, go and talk to him or her first; it would not be right for me to hear your story until you have followed the commands of Jesus." You will squelch a lot of gossip and spare a lot of anguish through this act of obedience.

The story is told of a lady who gossiped about a neighbor and then discovered what she had said was not true. She confessed her embarrassment to her minister and then asked how could she make it right again? Without answering her question, the minister took her outside, cut open a feather pillow, and scattered the feathers to the wind. As they stood there and watched them float off into a hundred different directions, the minister then turned and told her to gather them all up again. She got the point. It would be literally impossible to retrieve all of those feathers again, and so it is with the words we utter in gossip.

Is there an alternative to the potentially destructive power of the tongue? Consider Ephesians 4:29: "Let no evil talk come out of your mouths, but only what is useful for building up, as there is need, so that your words may give grace to those who hear."

It requires more effort and godly control, but using your tongue to encourage those around you fits the purpose for which God originally designed this organ of speech.

Encourage one another with words that are helpful. When William Gillette, the actor, was a young man, he lived in a boardinghouse. He was studying stenography at the time, so he practiced in the evenings by writing down every word spoken in conversation by the other boarders.

In referring to this experience, Mr. Gillette once told a friend, "Years later I went over my notebooks and found that in four months of incessant conversation, no one had said anything that made any difference to anybody."[2]

Do not let that happen to you. Make your conversations meaningful.

Encourage one another with words that are wholesome. Use words to build up, not tear down. The tongue should not be employed to communicate in vulgar, crass terms. It requires no intelligence and a very small vocabulary to curse. The only byproduct of such crude speech is a lowered esteem in the minds of those who are forced to listen to you. Let every word and figure of speech be such that it could have come from the lips of the Lord.

Encourage one another with words that are faithful. The greatest words that can be spoken are those that point others to Jesus Christ. Peter Buehler was responsible for helping lead John and Charles Wesley to a relationship with Christ. He once said, "If I had a thousand tongues, I'd praise Christ with them all." Charles Wesley, indebted for his faith, expanded this stray comment into lines that became the well-known hymn, "O for a Thousand Tongues to Sing."[3]

James is right—the tongue is powerful. Whether its power is constructive or destructive depends on how we choose to control its use. This tiny piece of tissue and muscle really does hold the power of life and death.

Death or Life in Words

A careless word may kindle strife
A cruel word may wreck a life
A bitter word may hate instill
A brutal word may harm and kill
A gracious word may soothe the way
A joyous word may light the day
A timely word may lessen stress
A loving word may heal and bless.[4]

CHAPTER 6

Living Wisely: Being God's Friend
JAMES 3:13−4:10

James appears to have lost track of his initial concern about teachers (3:1) as he develops his concern about the tongue's evil. Now the abrupt switch to talk about true wisdom and his readers' lack of it resonates with the issue of teachers. In the ancient world, particularly in the East, the most fundamental attribute of a good teacher was wisdom. The wise were not necessarily people with knowledge or intelligence. The wise demonstrated perceptiveness about how life works and modeled a personal life worth emulating. These societies created, preserved, and handed down their understanding of wisdom in the form of proverbial sayings. Such sayings can be found in the book of Proverbs in the Old Testament, in Sirach in the Apocrypha, in the sayings of Confucius, and even in *Poor Richard's Almanac,* by Benjamin Franklin. Such wisdom, which in ancient times focused heavily on speech and the difficulty of curbing the human tongue, helps guide us in how to live our lives at the practical day-to-day level.

James invites us to think about wisdom's origins and sources and how to tell true from false wisdom. He broaches this topic at the very beginning of the letter, when in 1:5 he encourages those who desire wisdom to ask God for it. Here he expands on the other voices besides God's that seek our attention. He also raises concern about the contentious behavior of some of his initial readers, and the influence they accepted from false wisdom. The same thing happens to all of us from time to time. The only solution for this is immediate and sincere repentance.

This will put us on the path to true wisdom, true living, and empower us to control that evil tongue of ours.

Living by God's Wisdom (3:13–18)

James recognized that discernment of true wisdom– choosing the best course both when life is simple and when life gets tough– is the ultimate issue people face day in and day out. Unwise choices often present themselves to us, but at the point of decision it is not usually all that clear that the choice is not wise. To help us recognize true wisdom, James lists the basic qualities of false wisdom and of true wisdom. He wants to show that true wisdom will reveal itself to be from God because it is good for us. It makes our life better. It also makes us wise in ways that can be observed in the patterns of our lives.

For once, James asks a question and then answers it directly and immediately. He follows up in 3:14–18 with evidence to support the truth of the answer. The question (3:13) is, "Who is wise and understanding among you?" This indicates that James rated some of the original readers as truly wise. At the same time he knew others were not. He insisted that all should make it their life's goal to become wise. The previous context implied that the wise are qualified to be teachers and are able to control their tongues. However, a person's wisdom must be demonstrable in a "good life." That is "good" as opposed to the "evil" that characterizes the tongue.

The Greek word translated "life" normally includes automatically a person's regular conduct or behavior. So adding "works," the same word as in 2:14–26, emphasizes how vital it is that wisdom be seen in behavior. It also reminds us that behavior, in speech and deed, is intertwined with the validity of our faith in God. All of this corresponds with a proverb Jesus cited: "wisdom is vindicated by her deeds" (Mt. 11:19). The inclusion of "with gentleness" shows that James knew full well that actions are determined by attitude. This prepares the way for describing the traits of false and true wisdom primarily as attitudes. Fundamentally, a spirit of gentleness guides the actions of the wise. In 1:21 the NRSV translates the same Greek word "meekness," and names it as the necessary attitude for hearing "the implanted word."

Two synonyms of this Greek word follow in this context, one appearing in the list of true wisdom in 3:17 ("gentle"), and the other occurring in the key quotation of Proverbs 3:34 ("humble"). The latter one suggests that humility really is the fundamental spiritual attitude James believes we need to foster in our lives.

In James 3:14 self-centeredness is pitted against humility as the attitude that fuels the actions of the unwise. Two Greek words work together to characterize this attitude: those translated here as "bitter envy and selfish ambition." They will be paired again in 3:16 as contributing to community chaos. Both words describe a preoccupation with self, with little concern for the goals and needs of others. The Greek word translated as "bitter" here is the same word used to describe the "brackish" spring in 3:11 and may suggest a connection between what flows out of a spring and what flows out of one's heart. The gush of bitterness begins deep down and inhabits the activity that emanates from it.

Boasting and deception are paired as examples of the kind of outcome to be expected from a self-centered attitude. Perhaps James considered boasting to be connected to envy and deception to ambition. This would picture an envious person boasting to outdo people perceived as being richer. It would show an ambitious person employing deception to get ahead of rivals. James knew that some people really are like this. They think such conniving tactics amount to wisdom. However, James warns his readers not to fall into such attitudes and behavior. This is false wisdom.

The falsity of conducting our lives in such a manner is exposed in 3:15. This approach does not come from God. Its source is everything that is opposed to God. James does not use "God," here, speaking only of coming down "from above." This apparently provides a contrast for "earthly" things. James employs "from above" again in 3:17 to introduce his list of wisdom's attitudes and actions. Perhaps, then, James intends "from above" to contrast not just with "earthly" but with the entire spectrum of false wisdom. All types of false wisdom and knowledge are assumed to be "from below," making it "unspiritual" and "devilish."

"Envy" and "selfish ambition" are paired again in 3:16. These two negative reinforcing attitudes nurture behavior in believers that opposes God's purpose. God seeks to bring peace to our lives. Such peace should be especially evident in the community life of the church. It cannot appear there if envy and selfish ambition characterize its members. "Disorder" describes a situation that is not fixed or settled. It refers to "insurrections" (Lk. 21:9), "riots" (2 Cor. 6:5), and "disorder" (2 Cor. 12:20). First Corinthians 14:33 highlights its presence in the church. Paul addressed a church whose worship was simply chaos and gave them a crucial underlying principle: "God is a God not of disorder but of peace." James assumed the same principle.

"Wickedness" describes something or someone as inferior or substandard. It commonly describes a swath of bad behavior deriving from a vulgar person of no account (compare Jn. 3:20; 5:29; Rom. 9:11; 2 Cor. 5:10; Titus 2:8; Jas. 3:16). "Every kind" brands "disorder" and "wickedness" as the joint source of behavior that troubles human relationships. These twin evils create the ongoing dysfunction of the church described and condemned in 4:1–4.

James 3:17 turns from false wisdom and its behavior to list true wisdom's identifying characteristics. True wisdom comes "from above," that is from God. James provided eight representative traits of such wisdom. In contrast to his treatment of false wisdom, James does not add any comment on true wisdom.

"Pure" is listed first as an intentional contrast to "envy" and "selfish ambition." The term refers to that which belongs to God and is holy. The original Greek word often appears as a New Testament virtue (2 Cor. 7:11; 11:2; Phil. 4:8; 1 Tim. 5:22; Titus 2:5; Jas. 3:17; 1 Pet. 3:2; 1 Jn. 3:3). Here it describes an attitude unadulterated by evil thoughts. "Peaceable" contrasts with the disorder created by envy and selfish ambition. Hebrews 12:11 is the only other New Testament occurrence of the original Greek word. "Gentle" is a translation of a different Greek word for "gentleness" than that used in 3:13. It is used also in Philippians 4:5; 1 Timothy 3:3; Titus 3:2; and 1 Peter 2:18.

"Willing to yield" is only used here in the New Testament. It suggests a person who is compliant to others in authority. "Mercy" repeats the term used twice in 2:13. "Good fruits" is reminiscent of Jesus' teaching in Matthew 7:17–18, that good trees must bear good fruit.

The final two traits have negative prefixes and name crucial, observable behavior that is the wise product of these wise attitudes. The Greek word tranaslated "without a trace of partiality" is the antonym of the related word translated "made distinctions" in 2:4. It means to not be judgmental or divisive, and thus to be impartial. It calls for actions that embrace other people without cultural, economic, or social prejudice.

"Without a trace of hypocrisy" negates the word *hypocritical* and describes people whose behavior is consistent with their stated attitudes. This is critical to James's teaching in 1:22–25 and 2:14–26.

James 3:18 concludes with a curious proverb. Intended to function as a motto over the lives of people who are wise, it emphasizes that those who are wise will conduct themselves in a peaceful manner. The NRSV translation handles this well (in contrast with the NIV), though the alternate reading, "by those who make peace," is preferable to "for those who make peace," adopted as the primary translation. "Harvest" translates the word for "fruit" found in the phrase "good fruit," in 3:17. This connection may be what spurred James to include the proverb. Key to understanding the proverb is recognizing that, at least here in James, the "harvest," or "fruit of righteousness," is in fact wisdom itself. This is wisdom in the very concrete sense of a person who behaves wisely. Such a wise person exemplifies the good conduct taught in the wisdom literature and schools, and particularly in James.

"In peace" describes the attitude or appropriate manner of a wise person. Making "peace" describes the work or overall behavioral product of a wise person. Peace, then, is the summarizing characteristic, trait, and outcome of the true wisdom that comes from God. The simplicity of this should prove helpful for those of us who sincerely wish to be wise. It will also enable us to identify for ourselves and for the church those who portray themselves as wise but truly are not.

Choosing Friendship with God over Friendship with the World (4:1–4)

James has laid out two contrasting options to inform our daily course of actions–God's wisdom versus the wisdom "not from God." James now challenges us to choose God as our wise counselor and not anything or anyone else. At this point James's comments stem from poignant knowledge of the divisive actions of some of his readers. He dissects both their actions and their attitudes to reveal them for who they are, persons living lives antithetical to the God to whom they claim allegiance.

James 4:1 pinpoints a serious problem among James's original readers by asking two probing questions, the second question actually answering the first. By using military expressions, James dramatizes the seriousness of the verbal skirmishes within the Christian community. "Fights and quarrels" (NIV) literally refer to "wars" and "battles." James depicts the true war occurring at the spiritual level within each individual involved. "Cravings" for James represents the intense desire for self-indulgent pleasure. The Greek word comes into English as *hedonism*. Coming from "within you," they do not delight God. Instead, they conquer the godly longings of humility that promote peace. Wisdom loses out to selfishness.

James 4:2 describes how the unhealthy success of pleasure within works itself out in damaging ways in the community. The first example is intended to jump off the page at us. Murder! In the Christian community? Yet, doesn't Jesus suggest in Matthew 5:21–22 that anger which expresses itself in demeaning words is tantamount to murder? James simply depicts a similar spiritual truth. Hedonistic cravings can make people envious of what other people have. This can eventually lead them to loathe others for what they have–material things, success, or power. This loathing finally manifests itself in mean-spirited words that intend to and do hurt others.

Can it lead further to the deadly act itself? It is tempting for us to ignore James's point as a big exaggeration, but James 3:8 has already assumed the association between harmful speech and murder. This association has a substantial base in the Old Testament (Job 20:12; Ps. 10:7–10; 64:4–6; Jer. 9:8). Words like slander and perjury are routinely depicted as bloodthirsty, physical violence against others. Proverbs 12:6, says, "The words of the wicked are a deadly ambush," and Proverbs 10:6 reminds us, "The mouth of the wicked conceals violence."

James's second illustration shows the effect of this spiritual crisis in the Christian community. "Covet" is substituted for "you want something and do not have it." James clearly intended to evoke a direct connection to the tenth of the Ten Commandments (Ex. 20:17; Deut. 5:21) to heighten the reader's awareness that what was going on among these believers represented a serious breach of God's most basic expectations for people committed to God.

Not only does self-indulgent pleasure-seeking wreck relationships and fracture the church, it also splinters our relationship with God. This appears most clearly in the way it directly affects prayer. The effect can occur in two ways, noted in the later part of 4:3. We may simply quit praying because we are placing our trust in the pleasurable things we want, rather than in God who provides all good things we need (Jas. 1:17). Or we may thoroughly insult God's generosity by using our "prayer" to indulge our ungodly wish list. Almost nothing is a better barometer of a messed up spiritual life than a messed up prayer life.

James 4:4 lays down the gauntlet in the form of a shrieking allegation: "Adulterers!" In breaking the tenth commandment they have broken the seventh commandment, too. As in Proverbs 4–8, refusing to follow the ways of wisdom led them to succumb to the enticements of adultery. Cavorting with pleasure is a breach of our vows of commitment to God. Though it sounds shocking to us, calling people who have betrayed their relationship with God "adulterers," or literally, "adulteresses," has precedent not only in the Old Testament (Isa. 54:5–7; Jer. 2:2; 3:20; Hos. 2:2–5) but also in the New Testament (Mt. 12:39; 16:4; Eph. 5:22–33).

James picked up on Abraham's prototypical relationship with God as "friend" in 2:23, also a relational term more compatible with living wisely than the terms "husband" or "wife," which we might have expected to appear as the opposite of "adulterer." What began as envy and ambition (3:14) and then became "cravings," or "pleasures" (4:1), has now evolved so that it can be typified as "the world" (4:4), a term commonly associated as the evil opposite of God in the New Testament (see the comments on 1:27; 3:6).

James declares a truth that should govern the lives of every believer: Friendship with the world and friendship with God are mutually exclusive. To have any real relationship with our Creator at all, we must trust in God and seek the divine counsel daily. We must not listen to the world and its siren voice that seeks to elicit our most selfish desires. There is no middle ground. You can no more be friends with the world and with God than you can have two best friends, or two equally-loved wives, or two equally-loved husbands. Anything less than an exclusive friendship with God makes us God's enemy. We must commit to God, our wise friend, and choose to draw on this friendship daily.

Repentance as the Condition of God's Friendship (4:5–10)

Having diagnosed the problem in 4:1–4, James 4:5–6 provides scriptural support that points to the solution laid out it 4:7–10. Our difficulty is that, whereas the source of the second quotation in 4:6 is clearly Proverbs 3:34, the source of the first quotation has been notoriously difficult to identify. It will prove helpful in sorting this out to consider the easier quotation first and use this to help with the second.

The difference between what appears in English versions of James 4:6 and Proverbs 3:34 is accounted for by the fact that James quotes from the Septuagint (the earliest Greek translation of the Jewish Scriptures) rather than from the Hebrew text itself, which is the basis for modern English translations of Proverbs 3:34. The basic sentiment is found throughout the Old Testament (Ps. 18:27; 34:18; 51:17; 72:4; 138:6; Isa. 61:1; Zeph. 3:11–12) as well as elsewhere in James (1:9–11; 2:5; 5:1–6). Proverbs 3:34 is also quoted in 1 Peter 5:5. The quotation is followed by an extended appeal for repentance in 4:7–10 and so is introduced as proof of God's grace. This suggests that the primary purpose for the quotation centers on the second line, God "gives grace to the humble." This grace, or "greater grace" is that God forgives sinners who humbly confess their sins and repent, something James offers as a last-ditch effort to redeem the self-minded, arrogant, divisive pleasure seekers who have been exposed in the previous verses. Of course, it is also true that if they continue on as they have been, trusting the world rather than God, they can expect to reap the full force of God's opposition to them.

If 4:6 describes a "greater grace," then it seems reasonable that the difficult quotation of 4:5 must also emphasize some aspect of God's generous favor toward undeserving humanity, what we might label a "lesser grace." The NRSV translates "God yearns jealously for the spirit he has made to dwell in us." This might qualify as articulating an aspect of God's grace—essentially the love for all humanity and the divine desire to have a meaningful relationship with us. However, two problems must be noted. First, no Old Testament scripture even comes close to matching this statement, and the introductory formula James used inescapably indicates that he was quoting something. Second, "jealously" actually is the Greek word for "envy" (Mt. 27:18; Mk. 15:10; Rom. 1:29; Gal. 5:21; Phil. 1:15; 1 Tim. 6:4; Titus 3:3; Jas. 4:5; 1 Pet. 2:1). The Old Testament does refer often to God as "jealous" over Israel, because the nation stood in a covenant relationship with their God. Nowhere does scripture say God has "envy." Technically, being envious involves things that don't belong to you, and God is sovereign over all things.

Greek grammar allows both "God" and "the spirit" to be either the subject or object of the verb. A better translation places spirit as the subject and accurately translates "jealous" as "envy," yielding: "The spirit which he has caused to live in us yearns with envy." The first advantage of this is that it matches the sentiment and includes the key word *yearn* of either Psalm 42:2, "My soul yearns for God," or Psalm 84:2, "My soul yearns, even faints for the courts of the Lord."

Second, it makes clear that "spirit" is part of the human creature and not a reference to the Holy Spirit. Finally, it draws on an idea already alluded to in James 1:18 and 21, that God has implanted every human with the word of truth, which comes to fruition when the person hears the gospel. In other words, God has integrated into every human soul or spirit, perhaps via the "image of God" (Gen. 1:26–27), the capacity or desire to search for the Deity in order to be complete—a spiritual "homing device" of sorts. Third, the word *envy* is appropriately a human attitude, now directed toward something worth being envious of, a relationship with God, rather than pleasures, powers, or material things that have characterized the lives of those whom James has been criticizing.

Thus, James verifies through the authority of scripture his point that God stands ready to deal with believers who are invalidating their claim to a relationship with God by keeping company with the world. Even though they have made themselves God's enemies by their two-timing ways, God has placed within their spirit from the moment of their birth a deep desire to know and be in a real relationship with the Lord of the universe. This "lesser" grace, or "natural" (general) grace is God's fallback, undeserved grace for all occasions, believers and nonbelievers. God's "greater" grace, or "supernatural" (special) grace involves the capacity to forgive sinners who repent and is entwined with the gospel and the work of Jesus Christ. This grace is ready and waiting for those who come to Christ acknowledging their rebellion against God, or who come back to Christ after flirting with worldly influences. James details these two graces in order to offer hope and encouragement to those who wish to renounce their sins and return to God's open arms.

Having shown that God offers multiple levels of grace to deal with those who wander from their relationship, James 4:7–10 appeals to those who have become worldly in their orientation to make the break, repent, and move into a solid friendship with God. Then they can draw on the divine wisdom in the course of their lives. The section contains ten command statements, the first and the last—submit and humble yourselves to God—being synonymous, echoing the scripture cited in 4:6. Between these two, the other eight commands articulate various aspects of true repentance.

"Resist the devil" is the flipside of submitting to God. To be God's friend, we must no longer listen to the devil, God's adversary. Indeed, we must actively interfere with the evil results of Satan's work all around us. When the devil sees that we are moving toward God, who stands behind us, "he will flee."

"Draw near to God" draws a picture of us turning our backs on Satan and taking our initial steps toward God, with the parallel result that God will "come near to you." The parable of the prodigal son pictures this so well, with the father running down the road to welcome his errant son home.

The fourth and fifth commands emphasize that repentance includes taking action to clean up our trashed lives. "Cleanse your hands" dramatizes the outward changes that are required, washing off our sinful behavior, perhaps trying to rectify the damage we have done to others in our sin, with sincere apologies and action to make remedy. "Purify your hearts" focuses on the spiritual, internal cleanup that must occur. Our hardened hearts of sin must be softened to care for others more than for ourselves, and to love God. "Sinners" and "double-minded" are what we are until we take these steps of repentance.

The sixth, seventh, and eighth commands, "Lament and mourn and weep" seek to elicit an emotional response to repentance. Having come back to God, we look at the trail of harmful things we have done in our sin and are devastated. Indeed, we should be upset and should express this in remorseful sobbing as a crucial part of the release from our sin. Joel 2:12 calls for "fasting...weeping, and...mourning" in our repentance. Jesus describes "weeping and gnashing of teeth" for the unrepentant in their punishment (Mt. 8:12; 22:13; 24:51; 25:30).

The ninth command, "Let your laughter be turned to mourning," parallels the previous three, viewing laughter as a demonstration of arrogance and self-pride. Repentance is the opposite of this. "Dejection" is the appropriate response for someone truly repentant of a previous insulting attitude toward God.

Finding true wisdom in our lives, then, requires walking with God daily as a friend and drawing on God's faithful help.

On the occasion when we sadly forsake our Lord for the world, we can depend on divine grace to accept our repentance and restore us to the close relationship of "friends" that we previously had.

SERMON

Take the High Road

(James 3:13–4:10)

Early in the twentieth century, poet Robert Frost penned these classic words about two contrasting roads:

> Two roads diverged in a yellow wood,
> And sorry I could not travel both
> And be one traveler, long I stood
> And looked down one as far as I could
> To where it bent in the undergrowth;
>
> Then took the other, as just as fair,
> And having perhaps the better claim,
> Because it was grassy and wanted wear;
> Though as for that the passing there
> Had worn them really about the same,
>
> And both that morning equally lay
> In leaves no step had trodden black.
> Oh, I kept the first for another day!
> Yet knowing how way leads on to way,
> I doubted if I should ever come back.
>
> I shall be telling this with a sigh
> Somewhere ages and ages hence:
> Two roads diverged in a wood, and I–
> I took the one less traveled by,
> And that has made all the difference.[1]

James also introduces us to two ways–the broad road and the road less traveled. This passage is a study in contrasts: human wisdom or heavenly wisdom, humble attitudes or boastful attitudes, self-centered ambitions or God-centered ambitions, covetousness or prayerfulness, friendship with the world or friendship with God, yielding to the devil or resisting the devil, single-mindedness or double-mindedness, laughter or mourning, and the list goes on.

To live in this world is to be confronted daily with the world's wisdom, motives, and philosophies. How the follower of Jesus responds to such contrasts reflects the individual's personal relationship with God. In the tense, crisis moments of life, the world will see your true colors. James, in this text, confronted his church about their response, individually and collectively, to the world's influence. The verdict was not positive.

James usually speaks of the world in a derogatory manner. You may be thinking, "I like this world. It beats living somewhere else in the solar system. Nothing is more beautiful than a sunrise on a crisp fall morning, or more majestic than a snow-capped mountain range, or more refreshing than a barefoot walk along the beach." I am sure James might agree, but that was not his point. Instead, he drew a contrast between the Lord and the world. Listen to how the apostle John described it in 1 John 2:15–17:

"Do not love the world or the things in the world." (What? I can't love the rain forests, Niagara Falls, or the giant Sequoias?) Just listen: "The love of the Father is not in those who love the world; for all that is in the world–the desire of the flesh, the desire of the eyes, the pride in riches–comes not from the Father but from the world. And the world and its desire are passing away, but those who do the will of God live forever."

When the New Testament speaks of the world, its warning is not about the majesty of God's creation; its warning is about the world's enticements that would lure us away from a relationship with God. Life's contrasting choices present themselves to us daily. At each decision point God calls us to take the less-traveled road in response to life's circumstances. Not many do.

Respond to Worldly Understanding with Godly Wisdom (3:13–18)

These verses may make you think that James abandoned his instructional warnings to teachers, but this is actually a

continuation of that very theme. This passage has everything
to do with what the Christian teacher needs: wisdom! James
asks the question, "Do you think you are wise? Very good;
then show it!" Let the good deeds of your life humbly
demonstrate that you are a man or woman of understanding.
When it comes to our claim to be wise, words are cheap but
actions will tell the story.

Some deeds of history stand as monuments to human
foolishness. This expedition of the Royal Navy furnishes a prime
example.

In 1845 Royal Navy Rear Admiral Sir John Franklin
and 138 specially-chosen officers and men left England
to find the Northwest Passage. They sailed in two three-
masted ships with the daunting names the Erebus (the
dark place, according to Greek mythology, through
which souls pass on their way to Hades) and the Terror.
Each ship was equipped with an auxiliary steam engine
and a twelve-day supply of coal, should steam power
be needed sometime during the anticipated two- to
three-year voyage. But instead of loading additional
coal, each ship made room for a 1,200 volume library,
an organ, and full, elegant place settings for all–china,
cut-glass goblets, and sterling flatware. The officers'
sterling was of especially grand Victorian design, with
the individual officers' family crests and initials
engraved on the heavy handles. "The technology of
the Franklin expedition," says Annie Dillard, "...was
adapted only to the conditions in the Royal Navy
officers' clubs in England. The Franklin expedition
stood on its dignity." The only clothing that these proud
Englishmen took on the expedition were the uniforms
and greatcoats of Her Majesty's Navy.

The ships sailed off amidst imperial pomp and glory.
Two months later a British whaler met the two ships in
the Lancaster Sound and carried back reports to
England of the expedition's high spirits. This was the
last European to see the proud sailors alive.

Search parties funded by Lady Jane Franklin began
to piece together a tragic history from information

gathered from Eskimos. Some had seen men pushing a wooden boat across the ice. Others had found a boat, perhaps the same boat, and the remains of thirty-five men at a place now named Starvation Cove. Another thirty bodies were found in a tent at Terror Bay. Simpson Strait had yielded an eerie sight–three wooden masts of a ship protruding through the ice.

For the next twenty years search parties recovered skeletons from the frozen waste. Twelve years later it was learned that Admiral Franklin had died aboard ship. The remaining officers and crew had decided to walk for help. Accompanying one clump of bodies were place settings of sterling silver flatware bearing the officers' initials and family crests. The officers' remains were still dressed in their fine, buttoned blue uniforms, some with silk scarves in place."[2]

History is not the only source for such examples. One need not look far today to find a similar lack of wisdom. I recently read about an intern working in a business office who turned to a secretary and said, "I'm almost out of typing paper. What do I do?"

"Just use copy-machine paper," she replied.

With that, the intern took his last remaining piece of blank typing paper, put it in the photocopier, and proceeded to make five blank copies.[3]

Even strong Christians are not immune from foolish moments.

Kevin Miller, Vice President, Christianity Today International, writes the following:

I was flying from San Francisco to Chicago. Five minutes before takeoff from San Francisco, a gate agent from ATA came on the plane and said to me, "Get your bags and come with me." I got my bags out of the bin and followed her into the jetway and asked, "Why? Is this a random security check?"

She said, "The captain refused to have you on this flight." Those words would cut you to the bone, wouldn't they?

In the terminal, she pointed me to the black vinyl seats and said, "Sit there. A supervisor will come talk to you." After waiting for several minutes for a supervisor to interview me, it dawned on me why I might be in trouble. My friend had been ordered out of the security line and thus arrived on the plane much later than I. When he came on the plane, I asked him, "Why were you stopped? Was it your beady terrorist eyes? Explosives?"

Soon four uniformed San Francisco cops, revolvers on their hips, walked up to me. "Do you know why you're here?" A long interrogation followed. I apologized, admitted I had said something stupid, and commented that I just wasn't thinking.

"We've decided to let you fly again on ATA. The next flight out is not till 11:30 p.m. You'll get into Chicago at 5:30 in the morning."

Inwardly I groaned, but quickly said, "Thank you." The lead cop looked down at me and said: "You win the prize for Idiot of the Day."[4]

Kevin ended up staying in the San Francisco airport for nine and a half hours. He was interrogated by the police and lost an entire night's sleep all because he made a foolish remark.

This was an embarrassing moment, to be sure, but it does not compare to the irreparable foolish choices that we make daily. Cutthroat businessmen and women can be ruthless with one another when it comes to getting ahead in their careers. Families are destroyed when a husband sacrifices his marital vows for the sake of an affair. Long-term friendships dissolve when one friend betrays the confidence of the other. The need for the next drug-induced high drives an addict to theft, assault, or worse. Wisdom is often in short supply! The individual who clings to old grudges, struggles to forgive, or is intent on satisfying the selfish desires of the heart is not wise. People who are envious and self-focused will stop at nothing to fulfill their wishes. These kinds of imprudent goals, James asserted, are not from God but ultimately from the devil.

In contrast to the foolishness of the world, James 3:17–18 tells us about the wisdom that comes from heaven: "But the wisdom from above is first pure, then peaceable, gentle, willing to yield, full of mercy and good fruits, without a trace of partiality or hypocrisy. And a harvest of righteousness is sown in peace for those who make peace."

James chose sharply contrasting words to demonstrate the difference. "Pure" is intended to contrast with selfish ambition, and "peaceable" contrasts with the chaos created by envy and selfish desires. In contrast to the overall self-focused perspective of the world, James demanded: Be thoughtful, be willing to yield or submit, be full of mercy and good fruit, which is the product of good trees, remember? "You will know them by their fruits" (Mt.7:20). "Without...impartiality" or "without...hypocrisy" describes the embracing of other people without prejudice, and details the genuine nature of the person who takes God's road. This list encourages us to be considerate of others. In other words, think of the other person before you act or speak.

After a few years of marriage a wife got out her wedding dress and tried it on. Alas, it wouldn't fit anymore, and she began to cry. When her husband asked what was wrong, she sobbed, "My wedding dress won't fit any more." With little thought he responded, "Oh, don't cry, honey, we'll get you a bigger one." Think before you speak or act. Robert Frost's words come to mind again: Thoughtfulness is the road not taken. Unfortunately, worldly wisdom often wins out over heavenly wisdom. I like what Yogi Berra said, "Don't always follow the crowd. Nobody goes there anymore. It's too crowded."[5]

 ~ Yogi's right. Take the road less traveled. Use godly wisdom in response to the self-focused, grudge-harboring world around you. Do not lower yourself to the unwise actions of others; you set the standard; you raise the bar. Do not compromise your godly wisdom. General Robert E. Lee was once asked what he thought of a fellow officer who had made some mean-spirited remarks about him. Lee thought for a moment and then rated him as being very satisfactory. The person who asked the question seemed troubled. "But general, don't you know what he's been saying about you." "Oh yes," replied Lee, "I know. But I was asked my opinion of him, not his opinion of me."[6]

Lee took the high road. Only the wisdom of heaven gives a man such a gracious response in the midst of personal attack.

Respond to Worldly Ambitions with Godly Motives (4:1–3)

James became a little more meddlesome as he challenged the disciple to examine personal motives. "Do you know why you fight and quarrel?" he asked. Such battles are the result of impure desires, and those battles rage for priority in our lives. In Alexandre Dumas's novel *The Count of Monte Cristo,* Edmond Dantes was best friends with Ferdinand Mondego. This great friendship was destroyed, however, because bitter envy and selfish ambition led to a deep-seated anger. Mondego wanted the love of a young woman who was pledged to Edmond. His insatiable desire was greater than his friendship. He coveted the presence of this young lady more than he valued the presence of Edmond. Without reading, you know the rest of the story is filled with sadness, deceit, imprisonment, brutality, escape, revenge, and ultimately murder. When you are motivated by worldly ambition and desire, the end result is never pretty. Interestingly, the original Greek word translated "cravings" or "desire" is *hedone,* from whence we get our English word, hedonism, the pursuit of pleasure as life's supreme goal. This, of course, stands in contrast to God's wisdom.

"You do not have, because you do not ask," James stated. God is the giver of every good and perfect gift. Do you need something? Ask! James continued: "You ask and do not receive, because you ask wrongly, in order to spend what you get on your pleasures." God is not opposed to people having things nice, unless of course that is one's chief motive in life. Consider these verses from 2 Corinthians 9:10–11: "He who supplies seed to the sower and bread for food will supply and multiply your seed for sowing and increase the harvest of your righteousness. You will be enriched in every way for your great generosity, which will produce thanksgiving to God through us." I like the way the NIV states the last phrase: "You will be made rich in every way so that you can be generous on every occasion."

The desire of the world might be stated in this way, "I want so I can enjoy it for myself." The response God seeks from followers is a simple prayer, "Lord, provide for me so I can be a blessing to others." That is a rare motive in our Western culture. That is the high road, the road less traveled. It is also the road to God's great blessing. To be in love with the world will ultimately lead to ruin.

Genesis 19 presents a vivid picture of this. When God was about to bring judgment on the cities of Sodom and Gomorrah, the visiting angels helped Abraham's nephew Lot and his family escape the impending holocaust. Lot, his wife, and their two daughters received strict instructions: Run for the hills; do not look back. As they hurried to find refuge, Lot's wife must have had second thoughts because she stopped and looked back with a sense of longing. Immediately, she became a pillar of salt. I have a physician friend who surmises that the devastation on the cities was similar to an atomic blast. As she stopped and lingered, she was vaporized; all that was left was a pile of salt. Regardless of how it happened, this truth remains: She loved the world more, and it cost her everything.

When you become a follower of the Lord Jesus, don't look back longingly at the world. Be motivated by the desire to serve others, not the desire to indulge self. Self-service may be okay at the local gas station and cafeteria, but never in the kingdom of God. Take the high road, the road less traveled, and be motivated by the needs of one another!

Respond to Worldy Associations with Godly Relationships (4:4–10)

The late Fred Rogers, who played Mr. Rogers on television, said, "Life is deep and simple, and what our society gives us is shallow and complicated."[7]

James would agree. In this text he contrasted a relationship with the world and a relationship with God. You can't have both; to be a friend with the world is to be an enemy of God. To be in love with the world is to commit spiritual adultery against God. James held nothing back; he became very personal. I cannot help but wonder if James was reflecting on what Jesus said in Matthew 6:24: "No one can serve two masters; for a slave will either hate the one and love the other, or be devoted to the one and despise the other. You cannot serve

God and wealth." Or as James put it, you cannot love both
God and the world.

I'm not sure the world really understands what a
relationship is. I saw a billboard recently that said, "Caring
and forgiving…it's more than a credit card, it's a relationship."
The world hardly understands relationships apart from things
and the ability to acquire them. I have yet to find a credit card
that is relational. Just try missing a payment and see how caring
and forgiving it is!

Just being exposed to the commercial ads on television stirs
up one's materialistic desires. Do you ever find yourself
watching and thinking, "I've got to have one of those!" The
emotions and feelings get all stirred up, but don't trust feelings.
One of the first lessons I learned as a student pilot involves this
very issue. Feelings will deceive a pilot, especially when your
vision is obscured by clouds or fog. It is amazing how the mind
can play tricks on your reasoning ability while flying through
the clouds. A pilot must learn to trust the instruments. The
instruments are not subjective; they provide objective truth.
Even so, your relationship with the Lord is not dependent on
subjective feelings. Trust divine wisdom; your spiritual life will
depend on what is true, not on how you feel.

The world's goods are certainly enticing, and they may
bring a sense of satisfaction for a time. But they do not last! If
you think that is an overstatement, consider the fact that in
1998 more people in the United States filed for bankruptcy
than graduated from college. Do not trust your feelings; trust
what the instrument of God's truth teaches you. Only God
provides a meaningful relationship and purpose in this world.
It may be the road less traveled, but it is the only road worth
traveling.

Fifty years ago, British theologian C.S. Lewis described
happiness in terms that make even more sense today in our
commuter-driven society:

A car is made to run on gasoline, and it would not run
properly on anything else. Now God designed the
human machine to run on Himself. He Himself is the
fuel our spirits were designed to burn, or the food our

spirits were designed to feed on. There is no other. That is why it is just no good asking God to make us happy in our own way without bothering about religion. God cannot give us a happiness and peace apart from Himself, because it is not there. There is no such thing.[8]

If you had a homemade, deep-dish apple pie waiting for you at home, would you settle for a Twinkie from a convenience store? No cream-filled yellow sponge cake can compare with a fresh pie! Why settle for what the world offers when the God of the universe offers you friendship. Take the high road, the road less traveled, and walk humbly with God.

> I shall be telling this with a sigh
> Somewhere ages and ages hence:
> Two roads diverged in a wood, and I–
> I took the one less traveled by,
> And that has made all the difference.

CHAPTER 7

Warning against Insulting God
JAMES 4:11—5:6

What if we do not repent and rekindle our friendship with God? Well, we continue to go on as before, living in response to the world's "wisdom" rather than God's. We live in opposition to God, behaving in ways that seem normal in our communities but that anger and insult God. In this section, James connects three types of behaviors, common enough among nonbelievers, illustrating how people snub their noses at God's sovereignty over us all. These three are: slandering another person (4:11–12), planning the future without God (4:13–17), and leveraging social and economic success to the disadvantage of others on society's margins (5:1–6).

Becoming Judges (4:11–12)

Criticizing others is so easy, and for some perverted reason it makes us feel better about ourselves. This seems to be especially true when we share our criticism with others besides the one we are criticizing. Although James viewed this kind of behavior as problematic among fellow believers, "brothers and sisters," it really is wrong to treat any other fellow human this way. The sin is not just against the other person but against the God who made us all.

Three times James repeats "speak evil against," the key word in 4:11. This specific Greek word is only used two other times in the New Testament (1 Pet. 2:12; 3:16). Related words are found in Romans 1:30; 2 Corinthians 12:20; and 1 Peter 2:1, often appearing in lists of vices. It is a compound made up of a word that usually means "speak" or "talk," and a prepositional prefix meaning "against." It is often translated "slander," but seems to include the variety of ways in which people verbally mistreat others, ways such as gossip, slander, insult, and mockery. James 4:1–2 has already equated such behavior with murder. The Old Testament also consistently condemns it (Lev. 19:16; Ps. 50:20; 101:5).

James carefully adds "or judges" to the second use of "speaks against." Apparently he intends to remind us that Jesus condemned such behavior when he taught "Do not judge, so that you may not be judged" (Mt. 7:1; Lk. 6:37). This teaching about judging also appears in Romans 2:1; 14:4; 1 Corinthians 4:4; 5:12; John 7:24; 8:15–16. Equating slanderous behavior to judging is a critical bridge in James's argument that a slanderer "speaks evil against the law and judges the law." In terms of philosophical logic, James employs the argument of the excluded middle (or, if a=b and b=c, then a=c).

Interestingly, James did not argue that the slanderer breaks the law but that he or she judges the law. The latter is a much more heinous crime. The perpetrator assumes a position above the law, thus preventing the law, or a precept of the law, from being applied. For mere mortals to put themselves in such a position violates one of the signal truths of the Old Testament: The law originates in God, who gave it to Moses and the people, with no room for revision.

Thus, for any of us to perch ourselves atop the law to amend or revise it, or to ignore the law, is to shove God over, to reject the sovereign divine authority, and to assume a position that belongs to God and to God alone. When we treat speaking against another as perfectly acceptable behavior, James claims that we put ourselves above the law, plop ourselves down in a chair that only God can occupy, and come very near to blaspheming God by proclaiming ourselves God over the law and over our behavior. Reminding us of what he said in 1:22–25 and 2:1–26 about being doers of the word, he makes a slight change to insist we are also "doer[s] of the law." We are subordinate to the law and to God's Word that stands behind it. Our role is to obey God's law as a source of God's wisdom for life. God has never asked us to be judges over the law, and never will.

In 4:12, James makes perfectly clear what he is getting at. Without mentioning God's name specifically, we know who he means when he says, "There is one lawgiver and judge." If we should have any doubt who this is, he added, "who is able to save and to destroy." This mirrors a comment Jesus made: "Do not fear those who kill the body but cannot kill the soul; rather fear him who can destroy both soul and body in hell" (Mt. 10:28; Lk. 12:4). Of course, only God is sovereign over law, justice, salvation, and destruction, and how these apply to us.

James concludes his warning with a rhetorical question that nails his point. To speak against another is to judge. To judge is out of bounds for anyone but God. It insults the divine sovereignty over the law and its application. Thus, what may seem like a minor infraction—like gossip—is in fact the worst offense possible, slandering the holy God. The addition of "your neighbor" at this point is intriguing. Surely it makes a subtle connection to Jesus and his most memorable teaching: "Love your neighbor as yourself," found five times in the gospels (Mt. 19:19; 22:39; Mk. 12:31,33; Lk. 10:27), and two more times in the teaching of Paul (Rom. 13:9; Gal. 5:14). Speaking against another surely does not embody this golden precept.

Presuming the Future (4:13–16)

Careful planning is regarded as one of the keys to success in just about any human endeavor. Yet in this section, James vilifies people who plan ahead as sinfully insulting God. James knew that when we plan we usually presume an overly positive scenario, which builds on what is happening today and what happened yesterday. Many potential disasters lurk around our future plans, which we do not and cannot take into account, even if we try. The future is God's world. Only God is sovereign over the future, yours and mine. To presume that we know what God plans for this world is to step, once again, into God's position and insults God. Respect for God's future plans must be fundamental to our attempts to plan into the future. We must never presume we know what our Creator has planned. We must constantly turn to God for counsel even when we do not receive any revelation about any part of the future. We must always allow for unforeseen tragedy that might wreck our plans, because God has other bigger plans that do not include our success.

James 4:13 uses the example of businessmen or merchants to typify the way all people insult God in their planning for the future. James uses generalized language—"today or tomorrow," "such and such a town"—with no specific kind of merchandise or amount of profit expected. This signals the reader that the situation is hypothetical and not a reference to anyone specifically. To think this is aimed only at merchants, then, is to miss the point. Anyone who plans for the future without taking God's sovereignty over the future into account is presumptuous and insults God.

Notice how James 4:14 shifts from third person to second person. The "you" is plural, as are the rest of the many uses of "you" in the paragraph. The warnings, then, are to all who read James, including us. The goal in what is said is to puncture our inflated evaluations of ourselves and cut us down to size. Our views of ourselves and our plans easily get completely out of proportion to reality until measured against God's goals and priorities. God values each individual and has a place for each in the future set out in the divine plans. However, the world does not revolve around our will but God's. We must not forget that. To do so is to sin against God.

James directly challenges our ability to know the future and our presumption to act on it as if we do. The haunting question, "What is your life?" and its answer that we are nothing but a mist pictures us against the backdrop of God's creation. Against that panorama we are hardly noticeable, unsustained, insignificant, and temporary. We are blips on the screen of human history, not to mention God's eternity.

James 4:15 provides an approved alternative to what the hypothetical merchant should have said. This verse has made "if the Lord wills" a mainstay in Christian vocabulary for centuries. The same understanding is modeled elsewhere in the New Testament (1 Cor. 4:19; 16:7; Acts 18:21, Heb. 6:3). It is critical for you and for me to recognize that James expects us to do more than simply utter the statement and then do whatever we want. James wants Christians then and now to make it a daily practice to subordinate our planning to God's will. Not a day should go by when we do not acknowledge God's awesome power over our lives in thanksgiving and praise and ask for the ability and the humility to recognize and live by our Lord's plans for us.

James 4:16 shows that presumptive planning without regard to God, typified by the hypothetical quotation in 4:13, rates as boastful arrogance. And boastful arrogance is always evil. Once again, as in 4:11–12, the logic appeals to the excluded middle (planning without God=boasting, boasting=evil; therefore, planning without God=evil). James already signaled God's opposition to "the proud" in quoting Prov. 3:34 in 4:6. Biblical examples of this principle in action abound. Pride in what God has accomplished in and through us seems to be approved (Rom 5:2–3; 1 Thes. 2:9; Phil 2:16; James 1:9), but self-boasting without acknowledgement or awareness of God's role in your achievements disgusts and is an affront to God.

Finally, James 4:17 concludes with a principle that appears to come out of the blue. This verse provides one biblical definition of sin. James imported this truth and attached it to this warning because he believed those to whom he wrote already knew better than to exclude God from their plans for the future. James did not have to teach them that truth. He did have to remind them of it because they knew one thing and were doing another. This amounted to a double sin, knowing not to do it and doing it anyway.

Of course, the principle applies to many situations beyond this one, and for that reason it is a good principle for us to keep in mind. We will be held more accountable for what we understand to be obedience to God than for what we do not, which should motivate us to act on what we understand. As believers, we know not to plan without God. James's warning should encourage us to implement this truth we know into our lives. An individual who did not know this truth should know it now, because James has just taught us how important this is.

Cheating the Poor (5:1–6)

In this section, James comes on like an Old Testament prophet. He echoes the language of Isaiah 13:6, which warned Babylon, "Wail, for the day of the LORD is near," and of Amos

8:3, which vividly condemned Hebrew landowners who cheated their day laborers, "'The songs of the temple shall become wailings in that day,' /says the Lord GOD; /'the dead bodies shall be many, cast out in every place.'" The sentiment of judgment against the rich parallels what Jesus said in Luke 6:24, "But woe to you who are rich, /for you have received your consolation. Woe to you who are full now, for you will be hungry. /Woe to you who are laughing now, /for you will mourn and weep." Indeed, James already warned the rich of their precarious position before God in 1:9–11, accused them of blasphemy in 2:7, and insinuated that those who want to "make money" tend to insult God in 4:13.

Despite the sweeping tone of James's condemnation of the wealthy, it would be unfair for us to conclude that James intended to denounce every individual of substance. After all, Abraham was wealthy, as were some Christians mentioned in the New Testament. When 2 Corinthians says that not many were of noble class, it does not mean that there were none. James picks out the rich as a class, much as he picked out the merchants as a class in 4:13, so he could easily typify the point. This time his point is mistreatment of the poor. This parallel is confirmed by the fact that both 5:1 and 4:13 begin with precisely the same words: "Come now, you…" As in 2:7, James presumed that most Christians were among those who suffered at the hands of the rich.

James's description of the torment the rich endure bears some similarities to the rich man's torment in the Parable of the Rich Man and Lazarus (Lk. 16:19–31). The parable pictures the torment in the afterlife as a reversal of roles brought about by the mistreatment of Lazarus in earthly life. James, however, tells the rich that they might as well begin weeping and wailing now in the present because their punishment is so sealed for the future it can be described as already occurring. By describing all this with a perfect tense with present force, James forces the rich to look at their accumulated goods deteriorate before their very eyes and see their own fiery destruction. It is a gruesome spectacle presented with great literary skill.

We tend to think of wealth being accumulated in bank accounts, stocks, and bonds. In James's day, wealth was contained in what one possessed. Thus, describing wealth as "rotted" pictures the produce of their fields as wasted away, or what they might have stored in barns as worthless. This is very reminiscent of Jesus' parable about the farmer who built bigger and larger barns to store his bulging fields only to die in the midst of this effort (Lk. 12:13–21). Jesus closed the parable with these haunting words, "So it is with those who store up treasures for themselves but are not rich toward God."

Most people only had one change of clothes. The rich not only had numerous outfits, but fine robes and garments passed down as heirlooms. They could have exquisite clothing made out of expensive cloth, and they could demonstrate their superior social status by flaunting this distinguished clothing in public. "Moth-eaten" describes the fate most likely of a wool heirloom robe, but also stands for the all the fine garments of the rich turned to tatters.

"Gold and silver" were the bank account of choice for the wealthy in biblical times. These precious metals might be owned in the form in money (coins) or in ornamented furniture or fixtures decorating their houses. Technically, gold and silver do not rust. Rusting applies to iron products. James probably used "rust" because its color connects to "fire" as a hue of red. Picturing these as "rusted" clearly means to depict their being rendered worthless because the metal was not pure and so became prone to corruption. The "rust" rises up out of the metal as fire and leaps over to the "flesh" of the rich themselves, destroying them in a frightfully horrific death.

As the rich farmer in the parable, the problem was not just that they were rich. They hoarded their wealth, "laid up treasure," rather than investing it in the welfare of their community. James did not necessarily call for giveaways, but for expansion of their farms and business investments to create jobs for the poor. What they did not count on was that they were living in "the last days." This much-used biblical term always connotes the end of time and God's judgment of all humanity that goes with it. Whether it refers to our own death or God's actual final coming, this passage suggests that this accounting of our lives in the last days occurs at a time of God's own choosing, not ours. We must be ever ready.

To hoard wealth is presumptuous and contemptuous of God because in doing so people assume they know the future, specifically their future, and that their money somehow insures them against all eventualities, including their deaths. Not so, thunders James. This insults God and solidifies their condemnation in God's judgment. That is not exactly the kind of future they thought they had sewn up.

Calling the rich to attention once again with "Listen!" James relaunches his no-holds-barred condemnation of them. He lodges a specific charge of criminal action based on a well-established regulation of Hebrew law detailed in Leviticus 19:13; Deuteronomy 24:15; and Malachi 3:5. Laborers were to be paid at the end of each working day. Indeed, they were to be paid "before sunset" because each day's wage was needed for the next day's expenses, for food and necessities. Ninety percent of the people in the ancient world lived this day-to-day, hand-to-mouth existence. To hold this payment back for any reason inflicted unnecessary harm and difficulty on families, and so God deemed such action or inaction as a callous sin. James 4:4, in fact, draws directly from the language of Deuteronomy 24:15: "Otherwise, they might cry to the LORD against you."

James's addition of "of hosts" to "Lord" introduces a particularly ancient Hebrew military expression that indicated God's vast power or armies. James at least implies that these heavenly hosts stood waiting for God's orders to cut down the rich. In fact, in 5:5, the massacre of the rich is called "a day of slaughter," a direct link to the language of Isaiah 30:25 and to the depictions of God's final judgment in Ezekiel 7:14–23 and Revelation 19:17–21. Why did God muster such forces against the rich? Because God had heard the cries of hardship, suffering, and injustice from the defrauded poor. This is all pictured as happening now to emphasize the certainty of its occurrence in God's day of judgment.

Both the Greek words for "lived...in luxury" and "lived... in pleasure" refer to extravagant, wanton lifestyles. Though neither is related to the word for pleasure in 4:3, the idea that believers would be asking God for the goods connected to a lifestyle so condemned by God is chilling. The further description of the rich fattening their hearts in 5:5 is appropriately ironic.

Excessive and luxurious food is a component of a wealthy lifestyle. Though we would have expected to hear "fattening their bellies," fat hearts are probably intended to convey what we would mean today by "hard-hearted" or "cold-hearted." Their self-indulgent lifestyle made their hearts so thick that mercy and compassion could not penetrate them. Surely then, justice toward the hardworking masses could never work its way into their fat hearts.

The final charge against the rich, detailed in 5:6, is intended to jolt us. It functions much like the accusation against envious, slandering Christians in 4:2: "murder"! Once again the eye-popping language is not to be taken literally. It is a way of noting the seriousness with which God takes their crime. Lack of prompt pay is insidiously harmful to people so dependent on their employer, threatening the health and livelihood of people who deserve better. Employees deserve what they have earned through their hard work. The rich should see their success as God enabling them to provide jobs. God gives the rich their resources for the well-being of all the people in their communities. Providing prompt, daily pay is the least they can do in response.

"The righteous one" refers to the working poor who do not deserve mistreatment. In this sense, they are "innocent," having done nothing to deserve the treatment the rich dish out to them. "Who does not resist you" is a way of describing these working poor as having no social, political, economic, or legal clout. They have no way of countering their mistreatment, except for complaining to God. James's whole point is that God does, indeed, hear their cries and will most certainly answer by punishing and condemning their abusers.

The peculiar language in 5:6 makes us wonder if James intends a connection to the trial and crucifixion of Jesus at the hands of those in power. That this is stated in the singular makes the possibility particularly intriguing. That Jesus identified with the misery of the poor and downtrodden in his ministry is unmistakable. Jesus' lack of providing a defense at his trial became a focal point for New Testament writers. It is taken as a sign of his innocence, his giving up of his life voluntarily, and as an example for Christians who continue to suffer because of their faith or just because of their social dislocation. So, it is possible that James intended for us to see all this. For us to affirm this absolutely, a further clarifying statement would have been helpful.

James was not expecting the rich to give handouts to the poor, nor was he condemning the rich for being rich. Rather, James expected the rich to provide jobs and adequate, timely pay for their employees. This lays an obligation on any of us, then, who employ others for any reason—part-time work around the house, babysitting, working in a privately-owned business, or holding a position with a major company. Whenever we employ another person, we face an obligation to God to compensate our workers fairly. Those who have the means to do so should also—recognizing God's control of the future—use the profit God has provided to invest in future growth potential for the benefit of everyone. To do less than this is to operate as if God is not watching and to insult God and the value the Creator places on every human being.

SERMON

A New Perspective
(James 4:11—5:6)

The relevant nature of James's writing never ceases to amaze me. Twenty centuries have passed since he wrote to the church, but the contents of this letter are as current as if he posted it on his Web site this morning. Our world has changed dramatically in the last quarter of a century; the perspectives within our society are shifting continually. The Word, however, calls us back to God's unwavering perspective—an outlook that will change the way we live.

A Godly Perspective on Finding Fault (4:11-12)

It is easy to skim over this text without realizing how much it speaks to us today. The word *slander* probably doesn't pop up in most people's vocabulary on a daily basis, so perhaps it does not apply to our current culture? Many of you may assume wrongly that this word is limited to some libelous statement or accusation. In truth, it is far broader in its scope, meaning to falsely accuse or to speak evil against another person. It encompasses any speech that demeans and belittles another, whether true or false.

Most of us guard against sharing what we know is untrue, but we show little reserve in sharing the truth, no matter how painful or destructive it may be. Richard J. Needham of the *Toronto Globe and Mail* wrote, "The man who is brutally honest enjoys the brutality quite as much as the honesty. Possibly more."[1]

We have no right to share something painful about someone else. To do so is to place ourselves above the law of God. That is a serious indictment. Speaking against another always tarnishes one's ability to reflect the image of Christ. The famous German Lutheran minister, Dietrich Bonhoeffer, wrote, "The angry word is a blow struck at our brother, a stab at his heart: it seeks to hit, to hurt, and to destroy. A deliberate insult is worse, for we openly disgrace our brother in the eyes of the world, causing others to despise him."[2]

Unfortunately, this passage can be taken out of context to reinforce a skewed understanding of what it means to pass judgment. Let me explain. Suppose you have a friend, who is cheating on his wife. You go to him privately, and in a spirit of love, you point out the error of his way. He angrily fires back at you, "Who are you to judge me?" Are you indeed guilty of violating this passage of scripture? Did you, in fact, judge him? After all, Jesus said, "Do not judge, so that you may not be judged." (Mt. 7:1; Lk. 6:37). When the word of God has declared an act to be sinful, it is not judging to warn a person about the potential spiritual fallout of such behavior. The distinction must be drawn between God's commands and human opinions. If you approach a neighbor who is washing an obviously brand-new car and say, "What idiot would buy a car that looks like yours. Don't you know that chartreuse and magenta look terrible on a car?" that is judging your neighbor (no matter how much you may dislike the color of the car). James rightly asks, "Who are you to be so judgmental?"

Reserve judgment for those matters that clearly violate the word of God. The bride of Christ has been deeply bruised by the scrappy fights instigated by opinions that do not matter. Several times in this New Testament letter James has reminded Christians to open their mouths only with care. Use your words to encourage and not judge.

A Godly Perspective on the Future (4:13–17)

Tomorrow looks just like today for most of us. We plan as though life will go on in the same manner indefinitely. James brings us back to a sense of reality with these next few verses. As we look ahead to tomorrow, we must answer certain questions.

What really matters in life? God does not discourage anyone from making plans. The Bible actually teaches us to plan ahead, especially for eternity. There is an old legend that supposedly comes from the ancient city of Constantinople. On the day the emperor was crowned, a stone-mason would present the new monarch with several marble slabs from which he would choose a tombstone. The wisdom of the day taught that the emperor should remember his funeral on the day of his coronation. Not a bad plan; we are not going to live here indefinitely. Determine what really matters, and make that the investment of your time and energy.

What is a realistic view of the future? Although we often act as if we can clearly see into the future, we are not clairvoyant. We have no way of knowing what will happen in the next sixty seconds, let alone what may happen tomorrow. If we could know the future, our fear and worry over the bad times would destroy any quality of life that we might enjoy in the good. God was wise to limit our understanding of the future. Since we only have this moment, we need to live it to the fullest.

James continued by saying that we are but a mist that is here for a brief time. Another word for mist is *fog,* neither one of which hang around for a long time. It's here and then vanishes. A fog seldom leaves a lasting impression. People in Indiana may talk about the great Ohio flood of '37, or the blizzard of '78. In our congregation we often talk about the church fire of '91, but when was the last time someone asked you, "Do you remember the fog of '86?" Vapors just don't leave a lasting impression.

A life apart from Jesus Christ doesn't leave much of a lasting impression either. Read the obituaries in today's paper—three paragraphs or less may sum up eighty-one years of the average existence in this world. That is not much to show for eight decades of living. Our lives are more like a mist than we can imagine. Tomorrow is not guaranteed to us. My family was returning home one evening from a day trip to southern Indiana. We were passing through a small Hoosier community when suddenly a car came flying out of a side street into our path. I literally stood on the brake and scrunched my eyes expecting to hear the crunch of metal. We missed colliding only by inches. After the intensity of that moment had dissipated, my legs and arms felt like they were filled with gelatin. I think we were spared a nasty accident by the grace of God in a split second. We had been talking and laughing as we drove along; everything seemed perfectly normal. Then without warning the scene drastically changed. Life is like that; we are here one moment and gone the next—a mist, a fog, a vapor.

Who is in charge? God is in charge! Life must be lived within the boundaries of the divine will. God alone knows what will happen tomorrow. To suggest that we are in control—even of our own lives—is to be guilty of gross arrogance and biblical ignorance. We can only anticipate the future. "Ask Marilyn" is a syndicated column that appears weekly in *Parade Magazine.* This letter appeared in the February 3, 2002, issue.

> If someone offered you a pill that made you immortal, would you take it? (The pill is free, has no side effects and could also be given to any number of people of your choosing.)
>
> BILL FRANKLIN, London, England

> The question, as I see it, is whether I would be willing to take the risk (for myself and for others) of eventually becoming trapped forever in a situation of intense suffering. This risk seems high, given the fact that we would be existing throughout every war, disease, and natural disaster that comes our way. Ultimately— someday, somewhere—we would be so badly damaged

that life would not be worth living, but we still would never die. So, no, I would not take that pill. No matter how long I could live happily, the prospect of eternal misery is too high a price to pay.

MARILYN VOS SAVANT

Her answer certainly gives credence to the necessity of putting God first and planning for eternity through Jesus Christ! I am grateful that the Lord is in charge and has a plan for our lives.

How should I live? To understand what is good and then not do it is sin! So live a good life because that glorifies God. Make the Lord your priority. Trust God with your future.

President George W. Bush delivered a powerful address to the faculty and students of Warsaw University in Warsaw, Poland, on June 15, 2001. In his speech Bush concluded by referencing the Nazi destruction of Warsaw in World War II.

Not far from here is the only monument which survived. It is the figure of Christ falling under the cross and struggling to rise. Under him are written the words: *Sursum corda*–"lift up your hearts"…"Lift up your hearts" is the story of Poland. "Lift up your hearts" is the story of a new Europe. And, together, let us raise this hope of freedom from all who seek it in our world. God bless.[3]

"Lift up your hearts" is also the story of the church. We can face tomorrow because God is in control.

A Godly Perspective on Finances: Be Careful What You Love (5:1–6)

When Hetty Green, known as the Witch of Wall Street, died in 1916, she was considered the richest woman in the world. She had amassed a fortune of $100 million, a huge amount even today, but especially for that time. She had more money than she could spend in several lifetimes, but was she rich? She divorced her husband because he spent too much. She sent her daughter to live in a convent because the nuns would pay her expenses. When her nine-year-old son Edward was injured in a wagon accident, she would only take him to the free clinics. Because of the poor care he received, his leg wound worsened. Eventually his leg had to be amputated, a surgery that could easily have been avoided. Her diet consisted mainly of dry oatmeal, onions, and cold eggs because she chose not to pay for fuel to heat her food. She lived in an unheated tenement in Manhattan and wore the same dress for years, during which it faded from its rich black color to a dull brown. She died worth millions, but she died alone.[4]

Was she rich? She had more money than most of us will ever dream of, but for my two cents worth, she wasn't rich at all. She lived the most impoverished life possible, a poverty brought on by her own impoverished spirit.

The affluence we enjoy in America often blinds us to the fact that being rich in the eyes of God is more important than any earthly wealth. Godly wealth has more to do with how we live than what we possess. In Revelation 3:17–18 the Lord condemns the church in Laodicea, the lukewarm church:

> "For you say, 'I am rich, I have prospered, and I need nothing.' You do not realize that you are wretched, pitiable, poor, blind, and naked. Therefore I counsel you to buy from me gold refined by fire so that you may be rich; and white robes to clothe you and to keep the shame of your nakedness from being seen; and salve to anoint your eyes so that you may see."

While the world equates wealth with success, God's perspective on financial matters is quite different. We become truly wealthy when we invest in a relationship with Jesus Christ. To know the Son is to be rich in the eyes of the Father.

Some people act rather foolishly in their quest to become rich. "Burglars in Larch Barrens, Maryland, were caught trying to cut through a safe using a Laser Tag gun from the local amusement center."

"Karen Lee Joachimmi, 20, was arrested in Lake City, Florida, for the attempted robbery of a Howard Johnson's motel. She was armed with only an electric chain saw, which was not plugged in."

The Ann Arbor News reports that a man in Ypsilanti, Michigan, walked into a Burger King at 7:50 in the morning, flashed a gun and demanded the cash. The clerk responded calmly that he couldn't open the cash register without a food order. The man ordered onion rings, but the clerk informed him that onion rings were not available for breakfast. The would-be robber left in frustration.[5]

Consider what James 5:1–6 has to say to those who are rich. In comparison to the rest of the world, nearly every American would be considered rich. There are degrees of wealth. You may not feel very rich as you pay your bills, but this passage applies to each of us. James probably addressed the wealthy land barons of his day. They controlled vast tracts of property and squeezed everyone in their employ to make a sizable profit. It is doubtful that many of these land barons were in the first-century church, but many of the laborers they used and abused certainly were. You do not have to be a wealthy land baron to be guilty of what James condemned in these verses, but offenses can stem from great wealth:

1. Hoarding is condemned. The ancient world had three standards of wealth: harvested grain, rich clothing, precious metals and jewels. James pointed out that hoarding is detrimental to all three. Grain stored too long sours and rots. Clothing becomes moth eaten. Precious metals and jewels don't actually rust or corrode, but this poetic language reminds us that when these things are hoarded their value "rusts" away.

2. Hoarding is the antithesis of faith. To hoard is another way of saying that God cannot be trusted. Do not be confused; it is not wrong to have a savings account or a retirement fund. God's Word wisely encourages such a prudent discipline. Hoarding, on the other hand, is an attitude that exalts wealth, promotes selfishness, and destroys faith. Would you sense the need to pray, "Give us this day our daily bread" if you had substantial goods hoarded up? Why were the Israelites commanded to collect only one day's supply of manna in the wilderness?

God wanted them to depend on their Creator and Deliverer for their daily needs. Those who tried to collect more, found their manna destroyed by worms. The person who hoards has no need for God's supply.

3. Cheating is condemned. Generally, wealth makes a person less generous and more inclined to cheat. When the rich and famous are caught shoplifting, we are puzzled. Do they not have enough money to buy whatever they want? Having enough is never the issue; wealth seldom makes one proportionately more free-hearted or generous. Charles Dickens' character, Ebenezer Scrooge, epitomizes that stingy attitude in Dickens' *Christmas Carol.* Scrooge had more than he could spend in a lifetime, but that only drove him to acquire more, even at the expense of Bob Cratchit.

The spiritual hypocrisy of the wealthy was one of the reasons that one-time theology student and evangelist Vincent Van Gogh gave up the faith and turned to painting. He decided that only in his artistic endeavors could he find beauty and meaning in this world.[6]

If you are an employer, do your best to treat your employees fairly and generously. Give freely to aid the care of the needy in your community. Give back to God and God's church to advance the work of the gospel. When you give, God will bless you with a sense of joy and fulfillment. You may remember the lyrics, "If loving you is wrong, I don't wanna be right." Sometimes we possess that same attitude about our material wealth. If loving money and things is wrong, I really don't want to be right. When that point is reached, God has been cheated out of God's rightful place and priority. When you feel yourself sliding in the direction of the stingy rich, ask yourself the question, "Who owns these things? Do they belong to the Lord or to me?"

4. Self-indulgence is condemned. Being rich is not a sin. Many men and women in the Bible possessed great means. Wealth is but a tool; however, lavish self-indulgence is not the tool of a believer. I heard this sage

advice years ago, and it has stuck with me, "Some love things and use people; others love people and use things. Only one is a godly way to live." How we view and use our possessions is an issue of balance: They are to be shared as well as enjoyed.

A few years ago our family enjoyed vacation time on the West Coast. We toured the San Simeon Hearst Castle, the opulent summer home of the famous newspaper magnate, William Randolph Hearst. The lavish surroundings defy explanation in words. I was dumbstruck by the fact that Hearst had provided a pay phone for his guests to make outside calls. Here was a man who had indulged his every whim and then some, but whose generosity could not include phone calls for his guests. James condemned such self-indulgence.

Our culture has missed the boat when it searches for success and happiness. It is not to be found in things, regardless how much commercial advertisements try to convince us otherwise. Perhaps you've heard the story of the man who was dejectedly walking down the street when he met a friend.

"Hey, Joe," the friend asked, "What's wrong with you?"

"I'm going through a tough time. Two weeks ago my great-aunt died and left me $50,000," Joe answered.

"I'm sorry about your great-aunt," the friend offered, "but why are you so discouraged?"

"Are you kidding?" Joe responded incredulously, "Last week my rich uncle died and left me $100,000."

"Again, I'm sorry," the friend reassured, "but what's so bad about that?"

"What's so bad about that?" Joe asked, "This week—nothing!"[7]

True success and happiness come from a relationship with the Lord who provides us with a wealth that cannot be measured in dollars and cents.

Like the sand dunes of northern Indiana, the world's philosophies shift and change with every wind that blows. Anchor your life to the unwavering perspective of God: Be careful what you say about one another, be careful how you plan for your future, and be careful what or whom you love most.

Chapter 8

Living Together in the Community of Faith

James 5:7–20

James concludes his letter to the diaspora church with a potpourri of sage advice. Scanning through this section, one does not discover a strong, centering theme. The opening "therefore" (5:7) connects to the previous section's theme of the Lord's coming to judge those, especially the unscrupulous rich, who insult God. If most of James's readers were among the oppressed, they could find encouragement here. But a warning is present for them also. James encourages patience in speech (5:9), honesty in speech (5:12), prayer (5:13–18), and reclaiming those who are on the verge of leaving the faith (5:19–20). The string that ties each of these sections together is our speech. This is an all-encompassing look at our speech patterns, covering speech directed toward God and speech directed toward others. James hammers home the need to use our speech, in all its variety, for the betterment of our community of believers. We do this as we bring wisdom and Christian maturity—rather than the discord of chapters three and four—into the mix of the community.

Patiently Awaiting the Lord's Coming (5:7–11)

The switch from addressing the merchants and the rich directly in the two previous paragraphs to addressing "brothers," or "beloved," as the NRSV has it, signals a refocus on believers, people committed to Christ. They are encouraged to exercise patience because they are among those the wealthy exploit. Their trust in "the coming of the Lord" is a crucial element in controlling their own temptations to seek revenge. Assured of Christ's return, believers can wait for the justice the Lord will mete out on their behalf against their oppressors. In the Old Testament, the idea of God coming in judgment one day is a broad theme. In the New Testament, this idea gets wrapped up in the return of Christ, an event filled with hope for believers (1 Cor. 15:23; 2 Thess. 2:1) and dread for unrepentant sinners (Mt. 24:37–39; 2 Thess. 2:8).

The first of three illustrations of patience, described in 5:7, focuses on what we can learn from farmers. The key point is not just patience but trust. Farmers trust in the climate God has ordained and continues to supervise. They trust God will make the climate as consistent as the Creator is. Only with such trust can they plant with confidence that their crop will yield what it should. For Israel, such trust and confidence was based on God's solemn promise to provide "the early rain and the later rain, and you will gather in your grain, your wine, and your oil; and he will give grass in your fields for your livestock, and you will eat your fill" (Deut. 11:14–15). From this James draws an enduring promise to all believers: we can be confident if we trust in God to grant us a fair reward, our "precious crop." Such trust must be more than a statement of words or a confession to a Bible study group. It must govern our attitudes and actions.

The two imperatives in 5:8, "Be patient," and "Strengthen your hearts," reveal that James was concerned that their difficult circumstances had made his suffering readers impatient. They wished for the Lord to come sooner rather than later so that their suffering might end, they might receive their reward, and their afflicters might receive their swift condemnation. James sought to fortify their determination to endure their conditions longer, but not indefinitely.

Note the contrast of the strengthened, lean hearts of the faithful (5:8) with the fat, weak hearts of the soon to be slaughtered rich (5:5). James assures his impoverished, abused readers that the day is near for them and for their afflicters. The New Testament teaches that Christ's return is always "near," or "at hand," because it can come to pass at any time (Mk. 13:32–37; Rom. 13:11–12; Heb. 10:25; 1 Pet. 4:7; 1 Thess. 5:1–8). Whether or not he comes tomorrow, we must live as though he may.

"Do not grumble against one another" (5:9) is the first in a series of commands that appear from this point to the end of the letter. It appears to emerge from the context of James 4. There, James dealt with the disharmony and verbal indiscretions of the community. Was this internal friction being exacerbated by their economic and social suffering? Or was this just a generalized warning calling on believers to build the community rather than tear it apart in preparation for the Lord's return? Probably the latter, since this whole section is moving toward generalizations.

The warning that their grumbling could result in their own judgment is serious. Judgment here presumes condemnation, as with the rich in 5:1–6. The afflicted, just as the rich, are accountable to God for how they deal with their circumstances. So are we all! This all goes back to the proverbial teaching in 1:9–11. The language appears to be influenced by Jesus' teaching: "Do not judge, so that you may not be judged" (Mt. 7:1). James's warning that "the Judge is standing at the doors!" may help readers recall Jesus' own teaching.

Christ is certainly the judge in mind, rather than God. This is evident from the immediate context, which concerns Christ's return, and from Matthew 24:33; Mark 13:29; and Revelation 3:20. All these texts picture Jesus as the one at the door. Such an image underscores his nearness, letting us visualize him about to enter the door. It heightens the warning to James's readers and to us to live our lives as though Jesus could walk in on us at anytime.

To this point (especially in 5:1–6), James has implied that his readers are suffering and abused without explicitly stating it. James 5:10 explicitly brings up the issue of suffering. This is a recurring theme in these concluding verses of James, emerging again in a different application in 5:13–18. Two biblical examples of patient trusting in the midst of suffering are provided.

The first example is extremely general, "the prophets." The Old Testament prophets often come across as loners repeating unwanted warnings and predictions of disaster if repentance does not take place. Jeremiah's experiences led to his being known as the suffering or weeping prophet (7:27; 18:18–23; 20:7–10; 26:13; 37:16, 21; 38:6), but other prophets suffered physically and emotionally. Just look at Hosea's marriage problems, Isaiah's rejection by the kings to whom he preached, Daniel's trip to the lion's den, or Ezekiel's exile and loss of his wife. James highlighted the prophets' "patience." Their patient trust did not focus so much on waiting for the people to repent. They displayed such trust as they looked to God to carry out the promises and judgments they had announced. The language of their "endurance" and being "blessed" harkens back to the beginning of the letter, especially to 1:12 but also to 1:2–4.

In 5:11, "endurance" is employed to link Job to the prophets. The Job example comes from the wisdom literature to which James is so closely related. The themes of patience and endurance are common in wisdom literature, but in the Old Testament, Job stands out in this regard. Job stands as the ideal archetype of the testing and rewards theme James painted in 1:2–4, 12. Job's story lets us see "the purpose of the Lord" and that God is "compassionate" and "merciful."

Testing through suffering is part of God's working plans for Job, for James's readers, and for us. It is balanced by the Lord's concern for our suffering and the certain reward for our endurance. Those of us not suffering economically and socially may find it difficult to relate to this principle by which God operates the universe. Is suffering required, or is it optional if we are to receive God's rewards?

First of all, we must become aware of believers who are suffering for a variety of reasons all over the globe and in our communities. It is possible that we can be used as an instrument of God's blessing in very real circumstances. Second, as emphasized in discussing 1:2–4, life at any level, socially or economically, offers its inherent difficulties and struggles. Each of us must view the trials that each day or each year presents us as opportunities God desires us to use for our spiritual growth. Through them we can experience the compassion and blessing God has promised to give us.

Speaking with Honesty (5:12)

It seems odd that this verse begins with "above all." "Above all" in reference to what, we ask? All wisdom? Everything advised in the book so far? In preparation for the Lord's coming in judgment? In suffering? The most prominent objects in mind here are the warnings strung together strung together since 4:11 about how we talk: no slander (4:11–12), no boastful planning (4:13–16), no complaining about others (5:9). In this context, then, the most offensive form of speech occurs as people swear oaths in God's name. James labeled this as dishonest or misleading speech. It implies God's assurance, thus making God appear complicit in our lie. This is the worst form of blasphemy. The coming of the Lord in judgment hangs over this warning as it does over the immediate context of 5:7–11.

We should not misunderstand what James was talking about when he disdains swearing. This is not about cursing at God or using the Lord's name in vain, though these are not acceptable forms of speech either. This is about making an oath to the truth, as we might in court or in personal situations, to underscore our veracity.

The reference to "by heaven or by earth" tells us that the background to James's warning is the same as that of Matthew 5:33–37 and 23:16–22. Jesus condemned the common practice of the day. To underline the veracity of their promises, people took oaths. If they were unsure that they could keep the oath, they would use substitutes for the divine, holy name (Yahweh). Matthew lists some of the common substitutes, noted in the passages include: heaven, the earth, Jerusalem, the temple, the gold in the temple, and a person's head. Matthew 23 lays out the principle here: It is impossible to disconnect God from an oath substantiated by these things or anything else, because God is the ultimate reference point for all.

Jesus condemned this widely accepted practice of the day as nothing more than deceit. They made it even worse by involving God's name in it, even if not explicitly stated. No doubt James echoes Jesus' teaching here. This may, in fact, be another reason for his introduction of "above all"; this is the Lord's command.

The point for us today is found in the "let your 'Yes' be Yes and your 'No' be No." Believers must be honest in their relations with others, certainly within the Christian community, but also beyond. We employ different means of deception today, and such means will always be different from culture to culture. Certainly, communication takes place in expanded ways today—by telephone, e-mail, fax, print media, business memos, student papers. Regardless of the medium, believers are to abstain from commonly employed deception techniques. As we do, we provide people with the proper view of God's integrity and holiness. In this way, we implement the teaching of Jesus (and James) into our lives.

Cicero, the first century B.C.E. orator, perfectly illustrated the kind of personal integrity James had in mind. He told the story of a man in the early days of Athenian democracy. Called to give testimony in a trial, he was about to offer an oath when the jury protested that this was totally unnecessary for him. Cicero noted that this was because, "The Greeks did not want it to be thought that the credibility of a man of proven honesty was more strictly secured by a ritual observance than by the truthfulness of his character."[1]

As believers in our communities, we should endeavor to establish just such a reputation. The honesty of our communication should make the impact of Christianity on our lives and in our conduct with others widely known and evident to all who know us or come into contact with us.

Praying Confidently (5:13–18)

James hooks this invitation to communication with God to the suffering theme introduced in 5:7. He was particularly interested in connecting to the motif of the Lord's mercy and compassion mentioned in 5:11. When we are in difficult circumstances as Job was, honest prayer like his provides us access to God's care, protection, and help. However, prayer is appropriate beyond just desperation. All good things in our lives are from God (1:17). Thus, when conditions in our lives make us "cheerful," prayers of thanksgiving and songs of praise are equally important responses to God.

The reference to "among you" suggests that James was not thinking primarily of private, personal prayers, but of prayers within the believing community. This corporate sense of what is envisaged is reinforced as other forms of communication to God are advocated in this section.

In 5:14, the general advice narrows to those in the Christian community who are suffering physically due to sickness. In this case the appropriate prayer is that of the community on behalf of the sufferer. This is carried out through the church's designated representatives, the elders. The New Testament does not fully describe the role of the elders in the early church. What is clearly stated is they were to be highly regarded men of character who knew the gospel well enough to explain it and defend it in light of false teaching (Titus 1:6). They were to take care of or shepherd the believing community in general. Only here does the New Testament mention this specific role of care for the sick.

The exact function of the oil is immaterial to the success of the prayer. It simply describes a common Jewish custom that continued to be practiced by early Christians. "Oil" is applied as medicine in Luke 10:34 and is associated with healing in Mark 6:13. Beyond this, oil is connected with spiritual dedication to God (Ex. 29:7; 40:9; 1 Sam. 16:3; Heb. 1:9). Roman Catholicism views this verse as foundational for the deathbed sacrament of extreme unction. This interpretation properly detects from the context that the people in question are so seriously ill that they are confined to bed at home. But it misses the whole point of the passage. The passage deals with life, not death! James anticipated that the prayers of the elders would contribute to the person's restoration to health. The anointing oil is applied "in the name of the Lord." That is the point of the passage. Prayer and anointing dedicate the ailing person to God's healing power, not to the power of human ritual.

In 5:15, "the prayer of faith" is intended to refer us back to 1:5–7 and the big difference between the effectiveness of trusting prayer and doubting prayer. The language of "save" in this context must refer to being delivered from the physical ailment in question, though a spiritual condition may be an aspect of the sickness. The separate clause speaks of "anyone who has committed sins." For some, then, a spiritual issue must be dealt with in relationship to their illness: They must "be forgiven" by God.

The following verse also assumes a possible relationship between serious physical ailments and sin. This belief is rooted in the healings of Jesus. In John 9 Jesus could vehemently deny the Jewish leaders' claim that the man born blind was the result of his or his parents' sin, debunking a common assumption of that day. On the other hand, Jesus prayed for forgiveness of sins regarding the paralytic (Mk. 2:1–12). He cast out demons as the remedy for some ailments, too. This connection is further assumed when the man in 1 Corinthians 5:5 is handed over to Satan "for the destruction of the flesh" and when 1 Corinthians 11:27–30 assumes that sickness and even death are the result of unconfessed sin toward others in the community.

James apparently viewed grave illness as another form of suffering in which trusting endurance is required. It is a kind of spiritual trial that God will reward if we handle it well. Remember that Job suffered physically in his trial.

On the practical side, this means that pastoral care of the sick, whether by the elders strictly or by those on the ministerial team, should include opportunity for the ailing believer to confess nagging sin. The fact that people who believe they could die in the hospital so often have things to get off their chests suggests that this is a healthy procedure, both spiritually and physically. The direct connection between a person's emotional/spiritual state and healing is now thoroughly recognized in patient care. However, this is not a task doctors and nurses should have to undertake. This is a responsibility of the faithful community in its ministry to the seriously ill among them and beyond them.

In this context, the encouragement to "confess your sins to one another" in 5:16 comes across as preventative spiritual medicine to stave off sickness in the believing community. Dealing with sin and supporting one another in prayer contributes to the physical and spiritual well-being of each member.

Much of our corporate prayer activity in churches today continues to focus on those who are suffering physically, and this is a good thing, an embodiment of James's teaching. What we don't implement so well today is confession of sin "to one another." Some churches incorporate a general prayer of confession into their worship. To fulfil this need, Roman Catholics provide for the sacrament of confession to priests as God's representatives. Many churches see small group studies, discipleship and mentoring efforts, and just personal friendships as better, less formal ways to encourage us to share troubling sin with others and receive help.

When 5:16 proclaims the effectiveness of prayer, the word *righteous* should not make us think that what is in mind is some kind of elite corps of prayer warriors who are somehow better than others. Rather, it assumes that all believers who have a relationship with God fit into this category of "righteous." This becomes clearer when Elijah is promoted as an example of an effective prayer in 5:17, with the emphasis that he is a person "like us."

James recounted a story about Elijah's prayer power. As we read, Elijah's more prominent prayer successes come quicker to mind—his spectacular prayer calling down fire from the Lord on a water-drenched altar (1 Kings 18:16–46) and his compassionate prayer to multiply the widow's flour and oil (1 Kings 17:7–16). James chose, however, to base his teaching on 1 Kings 17–18. In so doing he stated three reasonable assumptions from the story as fact:

1. Elijah prayed at the beginning and at the end of the drought;

2. the drought lasted "three years and six months"; and

3. "the earth yielded its harvest" afterwards.

James stressed the third assumption about Elijah's second prayer. This prayer led to divine restoration of the devastated land to its bountifulness. This fit well with James's interest in extolling the power of intercessory prayer to restore an ailing person to health, which initiated this teaching on prayer in 5:14.

Restoring a Community Member (5:19–20)

This very last section of James connects to the theme of restoring people in the believing community who are suffering. In this case, the suffering is thoroughly spiritual, and so sin plays an even stronger role. Again, the story seems to represent a hypothetical case rather than one to which James could attach specific names. James addressed his readers for the tenth and final time as "brothers and sisters." Here his purpose was not so much to signal an entirely new section of the letter, but to invoke language that encircled the whole community in what he wanted to say to conclude the letter. The repetition of "among you," as in 5:13, points to a connection also with what has been said since 5:13.

The individual has entered a period of spiritual crisis. Faithful resolve has been sorely tested, reaching the breaking point. What are other people in the community supposed to do when they learn about this? Not turn their backs and chastise the guilty party. Like the prodigal's father, faithful believers need to run to the one who "wanders from the truth," listen, counsel, and lead the wanderer back to full, trusting faith and complete participation in the community.

The Greek word for "wander" is usually translated "deceive" (Mt. 22:29; 24:4–5, 11, 24; Mk. 12:24, 27; 13:5–6; Lk. 21:8; Jn. 7:12, 47; 1 Cor. 6:9; 15:33; Gal. 6:7; Jas. 1:16; 2 Tim. 3:13; 1 Jn. 1:8; 2:26; 3:7; Rev. 2:20; 12:9; 13:14; 18:23; 19:20; 20:3, 8, 10), though in some contexts it means to lose course and go astray (Mt. 18:12–13; Titus 3:3; Heb. 3:10; 5:2; 11:38; 1 Pet. 2:25; 2 Pet. 2:15). It has application in navigation in terms of a ship going off its course and being lost. The concern that believers wander off into false teaching pervades the New Testament (Lk. 21:8; Gal. 6:7; 2 Tim. 3:13; Titus 3:3; 1 Pet. 2:25; 2 Pet. 2:15; 1 Jn. 2:26; Rev. 13:14). Such false teaching usually involves doctrinal error, but often leads to moral laxity. The Greek conditional clause and subjunctive verb show that James was not overly concerned with any particular false teaching that faced or tempted his readers. He is presenting a hypothetical case, as he does so often.

The "truth," as elsewhere in the New Testament, probably means the truth of the gospel, that is, the essential message of

Christ. It retains implications for Christian conduct, both communal and individual. Some people commit themselves to Christ and his community. Then for some reason they become less committed to the values of the community or to the claims of Christ. Such people are "wander[ing] from the truth." They are "drifting away," or "backsliding," as we sometimes say. Who knows what causes people to do this. An infinite variety of personal, physical, family, ethical, and theological crises can cause people quietly to disengage themselves from us.

James makes it perfectly clear that one of our most important responsibilities as a Christian community is to take care of people in these situations in ways that bring them back. Is this the job of the elders or the ministerial team on our behalf? James did not see it that way. He writes, "whoever brings back a sinner from wandering." We all have the responsibility to watch out for one another and take action as needed. James emphasizes the serious nature of this responsibility by showing the results accomplished: We "will save the sinner's soul from death." The death in mind is the spiritual death of condemnation and judgment by God. If not stopped, such a person will leave Christ and lose salvation.

By rescuing a fellow community member from spiritual death you will "cover a multitude of sins." However far people might wander from the truth of Christ and however much or grievously they might sin against God, they can be restored to full participation in the faithful community. It simply is not possible to wander beyond the coverage of God's grace. This is a crucial, comforting word that "wanderers" we might attempt to counsel must hear. If they have known the truth, their guilt for having left it may be the very thing that holds them back from confession and restoration.

Life is tough sometimes, and it can take a great toll on our faith. Part of the solution is to maintain a high resolve in our faith toward God, endure it, and move on with greater faith, as James emphasized in his opening verses. Sometimes life is so tough and our faith so damaged that we need help to maintain it long enough to receive the blessing from the trial. That is where we, the church, fellow believers in the community of faith, come in. We are essential to each other's spiritual survival. Each of us has a vital role to play for others in our faithful community, just as others do for us. We need to take this responsibility seriously and not hesitate to rescue one another from spiritual and everlasting disaster.

Sermon One

Rich in Virtues
(James 5:7–12)

Certain spiritual virtues are far more valuable than any wealth the world can offer. Riches cannot sustain an individual in the difficult circumstances of life, but these godly virtues can. When you are feeling emotionally bankrupt, these virtues bring their rich rewards.

Be Patient (5:7–8)

Patience will never be known as an American virtue. We twenty-first century Americans are perhaps the least patient people on the face of the earth! When life is hard, that is when it is most difficult to be patient. The anonymous Native American proverb reminds us, "The soul would have no rainbow if the eye had no tears." When life is at its worst, God will sustain and bless, if we are patient. The farmer must patiently wait for the seasons to work their magic on the seed so that the crop will be ready for harvest. What happens to the farmer who can't wait, and tries to harvest his corn before it tassels? He gets nothing. Patience always brings a harvest. As the story goes, Philips Brooks, the minister who penned the beautiful Christmas carol "O Little Town of Bethlehem," was pacing in his office one day when someone entered his study and asked, "What's the matter, preacher?" Frustrated, Brooks replied, "I'm in a hurry, and God isn't." Be patient! God's timing is always perfect![2]

Be Positive (5:9)

It had been a long, turbulent flight. The passengers were tired of the rough ride, and the landing was even worse. As the passengers exited the plane, the captain stood by the cockpit door to thank them for choosing to fly with their airline. The pilot dreaded this because of the unusually hard landing. Surprisingly, the people filed off, and no one said a word, until the last passenger, an elderly lady. As she stood in front of the captain, she glared and said, "Can I ask a question?" "Sure" answered the captain. The lady continued, "Did we land, or were we shot down?"

Not a week goes by without my witnessing the brutality of someone's negative manner. Families are hurt, employees become discouraged, volunteers lose their motivation, and spouses feel like giving up—all for the lack of positive, encouraging affirmation. I don't remember where I first heard it, but it has stayed with me through the years: "When you help someone up a hill, you get that much closer to the top yourself." That proverbial statement is a good assessment of the value of being positive. Life is an uphill climb. If you are like me, you long for those refreshing summit experiences. I find myself constantly searching for a new way to the top of the next hill.

As Christians, we dare not make the climb alone! Being an encourager to others who are on the way up gets you there faster. Encouragement is an interesting commodity: The more of it you give away, the more you have left for yourself. A true encourager is one who helps other people reach the summit of life's experiences when they might not reach it otherwise. A true encourager gets behind and pushes. Why? Encouragers are more concerned about another's uphill climb than their own. A true encourager gets more excited about another's arrival at the hilltop than about being the first one there. Being an encourager is not an option in the Christian life!

In a world full of discouraging experiences and empty promises, it is so refreshing to meet someone who is an "encourager." I like the way Ella Wheeler Wilcox describes the importance of encouragement, "A pat on the back is only a few vertebrae removed from a kick in the pants, but is miles ahead in results."[3] The world is good at kicking, but I believe that God wants us, God's people, to be known for our pats on the back!

The book of Acts introduces us to a man named Joseph. He is only called Joseph once. The next thirty-four times we read about him, his nickname is used: Barnabas, which means son of encouragement. That is a great nickname. The early church concluded that his character and actions demanded a more descriptive designation than what the good name Joseph supplied. Those who knew him best gave him the nickname "Encourager."

If your friends, acquaintances and coworkers had to give you a descriptive nickname today on the basis of your words, actions, and attitude, what would it be? Not many of us would be given the name Barnabas. Yet all of us should be living in a manner that would earn us that name.

None of the outstanding qualities we find in Barnabas would be possible without the aid of God's Spirit. Acts 11:24 says of Barnabas, "For he was a good man, full of the Holy Spirit and of faith. And a great many people were brought to the Lord." Therein is the secret; be full of the Holy Spirit. When the presence of God is at work in and through you, you will be a Barnabas, too.

This matter of encouragement should not be taken too lightly. Do not consider this spiritual virtue to be some obscure biblical principle. In the New Testament, the word most often translated "encourage" (*parakaleo*), is found 109 times. It always describes a believer building up another believer in the faith, literally meaning "to come along side of in order to give aid." It carries the idea of "speaking to another in order to bring him nearer, either physically or in a personal relationship."[4] Biblical encouragement is not necessarily used in the same manner that it might be used today. Statements such as, "I like your car," or "You're wearing a beautiful dress," or "That was a great putt!" are not the kinds of encouragement we find in the scriptures. New Testament encouragement holds a much deeper meaning, referring to what a believer says or does to help someone else become a stronger Christian. It refers to one's responsibility to build up fellow believers. We dare not minimize the significance of such a biblical principle. NIV uses the word *encourage* or *encouragement* 63 times. Comparatively, baptism appears 83 times; repentance 55 times; and confession 18 times. The Lord's supper has only 7 direct references and is the subject under consideration in only 33 verses. This is not to suggest that encouragement is more important than or even equal to these weighty biblical issues. However, in light of the numerous references to encouragement, Christians must stop justifying their negative, backbiting, divisive, and critical treatment of one another in the Kingdom. God calls us to be encouragers!

Hebrews 3:13 says, "But encourage one another daily, as long as it is called today" (NIV).

Hebrews 10:24–25 states, "And let us consider how to provoke one another to love and good deeds, not neglecting to meet together, as is the habit of some, but encouraging one another, and all the more as you see the Day approaching."

First Thessalonians 5:14 exhorts, "And we urge you, beloved, to admonish the idlers, encourage the faint hearted, help the weak, be patient with all of them."

Bonne Steffen, editor of *Christian Reader*, reports a true story from a Florida middle school:

> A boy was always in trouble at school. When the parents of the middle-schooler received one more call to come in and meet with his teacher and the principal, they knew what was coming. Or so they thought.
>
> The teacher sat down with the boy's parents and said, "Thanks for coming. I wanted you to hear what I have to say."
>
> The father crossed his arms and waited, thinking what defense he could use this time. The teacher proceeded to go down a list of ten things—ten positive affirmations of the junior high "troublemaker." When she finished, the father said, "And what else? Let's hear the bad things."
>
> "That's all I wanted to say," she said.
>
> That night when the father got home, he repeated the conversation to his son. And not surprisingly, almost overnight, the troublemaker's attitude and behavior changed dramatically; all because a teacher looked past the negatives.[5]

Be Persistent (5:10–11)

Do not give up in the tough times. Persevere! Thousands of biblical characters and faithful church people have persevered before us; we can, too, if we do not give up. Walter Elliott writes, "Perseverance is not a long race; it is many short races one after another."[6]

James referred to one such character. Let me tell you his story, a man of patience and perseverance who in one single day saw his wonderful life simply evaporate. He may have been sitting on the back porch when an exhausted farm hand ran up and explained that a bunch of thieves had stolen the herds and killed the ranch hands. Only he had escaped with the bad news. Before he was finished, a shepherd smelling of smoke broke in and explained that lightning had started a brush fire. The whole flock had been destroyed. He was the only shepherd who had escaped with the bad news. Then a third breathless employee showed up with the news that terrorists had raided the camel herds and killed everyone except for him. Before the land owner even had the chance to process all of this bad news, a fourth man showed up choking back the tears, "All of your children were at your oldest son's house. They were having such a good time that no one saw the tornado before it struck the house. I'm sorry, none of them survived." I cannot imagine what must have gone through his mind: shock, anger, frustration, anguish, bitterness, discouragement, and more. Welcome to the story of Job.

No book brings suffering to our attention quite like the book of Job. No biblical name is more synonymous with perseverance than Job. And no book helps us focus on the ultimate mercy of God better than Job.

One of the common denominators of successful people is their ability to persevere. The famous American poet Carl Sandburg flunked English. The great inventor Thomas Edison did not do well in school; his teachers thought he lacked the ability to learn. Einstein could not speak until he was four and did not read until he was seven. Beethoven's music teacher said, "As a composer, he's hopeless." Walt Disney was fired by a newspaper editor who said Disney did not have any creative ideas. An editor once told Louisa May Alcott that she was not capable of writing anything that would appeal to a popular audience. Michael Jordan did not make the high school basketball team in his sophomore year because the coach said he wasn't good enough.[7]

I believe that God has planted the seed of determination in each heart; whether or not we cultivate that virtue is up to us. When life gets tough, you get tougher. When you cannot see the end of the road ahead, just remember, by perseverance even the snails eventually reached the ark!

Don't take yourself or life itself too seriously. Stay the course. God is full of compassion and mercy for those who don't give up!

After winning the gold medal for the long jump in the 1996 Olympic games, Carl Lewis was asked by Bryant Gumbel on "The Today Show": "You have competed for almost twenty years. To what do you attribute your longevity?"

Lewis, perhaps the greatest track and field athlete of all time, did not hesitate with his answer: "Remembering that you have both wins and losses along the way. Don't take either one too seriously."[8]

Be Prudent (5:12)

Guard your speech carefully. Be known for your prudence. Choose your words wisely! Truthfully, this has more to do with the reputation of your speech than with the actual words you use. This has nothing to do with cursing at God or using the Lord's name in a vulgar context, though such uses would certainly not be acceptable forms of speech. This is about making an oath to the truth by invoking the name of God, or the city of Jerusalem, or the gold in the temple—all of which involve God. In the exegetical section above, William Baker wrote the following:

> Jesus condemned this widely accepted practice of the day as nothing more than deceit. They made it even worse by involving God's name in it, even if not explicitly stated. No doubt, James echoes Jesus' teaching here. This may, in fact, be another reason for his

introduction of "above all else"; this is the Lord's command.

The point for us today is found in the "let your 'Yes' be yes and your 'No' be no." Believers must be honest in their relations with others, certainly within the Christian community, but also beyond."

Several years ago, Kansas State Senate Chaplain Fred Holloman opened a session of the senate with this prayer:

Omniscient Father: Help us to know who is telling the truth. One side tells us one thing and the other just the opposite. And if neither side is telling the truth, we would like to know that, too. And if each side is telling half the truth, give us the wisdom to put the right halves together. In Jesus' name, Amen.[9]

Be known as wise and prudent in your responses. Let your reputation be such that when you speak, there is no doubt as to the veracity of your words.

These virtues are better than money in the bank—be patient, be positive, and be persistent. It is not what we accumulate in this world that matters most; it is what we become that makes us rich. If you doubt that truth, consider this observation: "The main emotion of the adult American who has had all the advantages of wealth, education, and culture is disappointment."[10] Earthly wealth apart from a relationship with Jesus Christ brings emptiness. So fill your life with the pleasing virtues of God, not the void of possessions.

SERMON TWO

It's a Matter of Prayer
(James 5:13–20)

As late as the fall of 2003 the team at www.newprayer.com was helping transmit prayer to God. At least, that is what the creators of this Web site were advocating. Crandall Stone, at the age of forty-nine, set up the Web site in 1999 after a night of drinking and philosophizing with some friends in Vermont.

The engineer and freelance consultant from Cambridge, Massachusetts, chipped in with his friends to build a $20,000 radio-wave-transmitting Web site. Believing that God was out there somewhere, they consulted with NASA scientists to determine where the Big Bang originated. Upon their discovery that a star cluster called M13 was the oldest known part of the universe, they aimed the Web site antennas to that location. Of the free service, Stone said, "It appears that most people take our service seriously and that a large number are gratified by the results." They transmitted about fifty thousand prayers a week from people all around the world toward M13, in the hope that the God of the universe would hear them. By January 2004 the Web site address www.newprayers.com was up for sale. God is still answering prayer the old fashioned way.

The apostle James did not have a Web site, but what he offered is far better. It is a simple but practical lesson on reaching the ears of God with our prayers. Prayer is one of the most common of Christian virtues. People who are not even religious understand the meaning of prayer. They may have a skewed view of it, but they know it involves addressing God. Let James give you a fresh look at prayer and its priority in the Christian's life.

When Should One Pray? (5:13–16a)

When One Is in Trouble. Most people are likely to pray when they are in trouble even if they are only nominal believers. It has been interesting to observe that on the Sunday following any national crisis (beginning of the Gulf War, the disaster of 9/11, Operation Iraqi Freedom, etc.), church attendance increases noticeably. People want to pray when they are in trouble.

What do you do when you are in trouble? You pray. Most people in their crisis moments really want to believe that there is a God who will come to the rescue. In all my years of ministry, I have never had people refuse a prayer offered in the midst of a crisis.

Is God interested in your prayers when you are in trouble? Most certainly. Would the Creator like to hear from you at other times when you are not in trouble? Most certainly. A parent can easily understand that frustration. If you only hear from your children when they are desperate or in need of cash, it does not take long for that attitude to grow old. As a parent, God wants to hear from us in more than just the crisis moments of life.

When One Is Happy. In times of trouble, prayer is at the top of the priority list for the average Christian; in times of joy, however, prayer is seldom considered important. Why is there such an obvious dichotomy? Who needs God when he or she is happy? When all is well in life, we tend to forget God. Sometimes we rationalize our lack of spiritual discipline by suggesting that we are motivated by godly concern. Why should we take up God's valuable time when nothing is wrong? After all, God is busy with wars, famine, droughts, and pestilence throughout the world. Aren't we thoughtful? Truthfully, we are just thoughtless and negligent. It's not God's time we are worried about; it's ours. God isn't on Eastern Standard Time; God stays on Eternal Standard Time. The one who created time doesn't need daylight savings time; the saving light is always shining in heaven. God can handle the wars in the Middle East and listen to your thanks and praise for the joys all at the same time. I never tire of listening to my daughters talk about their happy experiences in life. God wants to hear about our good days, too.

When you pray in the happy times, keep it happy! Most of the time we are more like the proverbial little boy who concluded his short bedtime prayer with, "And now, God, I'd like to tell you about some things I'm not thankful for." It might be human nature to temper our joy with what is wrong, but it is not a part of the spiritual nature! Learn to pray without reverting to the bad news of the day.

You might notice that "happy" and "prayer" do not seem to be connected together in this text. Truly they are, but the phrase "sing songs of praise" confuses us. If one person prays the Lord's Prayer and another sings it, what is the difference? Singing praise is just another form of prayer. When I sing the old hymn, "Praise to the Lord, the Almighty, let all that is in me adore him," to whom am I singing? When I worship with the powerful chorus, "Shout to the Lord all the earth, let us sing power and majesty, praise to the King," to whom am I singing? To sing praise to God is no less important or sincere than speaking praise to God. The key is praising God both in word and in song. Pray when you are happy.

When One Is Sick. Too many see in this verse a mystical or magical formula for physical healing. This is a biblical pattern to be employed by the shepherds of God's flock as they minister to Christians in need, but it should never be viewed as the cure-all spiritual prescription. Consider this story.

Amy Carmichael, a turn-of-the-century missionary to India, described an attempted healing of one of her treasured coworkers. A woman named Ponnammal contracted cancer in 1913. Amy was, of course, aware of James's prescription to call for the elders of the church to anoint the ill and offer the prayer of faith. Still, she and her fellowship were not sure what to do. So they sought a sign asking that, if it were God's will, would God send someone to them who was earnest about James's prescription for healing? The person came, an old friend of Amy from Madras. As her biographer, Elisabeth Elliott, describes it:

> It was a solemn meeting around the sickbed, the women dressed as usual in their hand loomed saris, but white ones for this occasion. They laid a palm branch across Ponnammal's bed as a sign of victory and accepted whatever answer God might give, certain that whether it was to be physical healing or not, He would give victory and peace. It sounds like a simple formula. It was an act of faith, but certainly accompanied by the anguish of doubt and desire which had to be brought again and again under the authority of the Master... From that very day, Ponnammal grew...worse. The pain increased, and her eyes grew dull as she lingered for days in misery until she reached her limit and her "warfare was accomplished."[11]

No mystical or spiritual remedy binds God to our requests as if God were some healing genie in a lamp. Will I call for the elders to anoint and pray when a member of my family is sick? Absolutely! Prayer is always the right approach, but the answer must remain God's alone to grant. God can heal a person any time or any place; it's up to our Lord.

The oil was ordinary, but it was the best medicine of the day. In the last fifty years we have come to expect a medicine for any and every ailment. From antibiotics to antidepressants, a pill, injection, or syrup is out there to cure it. This has not always been so. The good Samaritan poured oil on the wounds of the beaten stranger he found along the road. It was the best that could be done. It's not been all that many years since castor oil was viewed by many as a cure-all. My grandfather used kerosene or coal oil for all kinds of cuts and problems, with amazing results I might add. Charles Swindoll writes, "James is simply saying that the elders should make sure we're getting proper medical treatment and pray for us."[12]

Here is another perspective on this passage. The word that is translated "sick" can also be translated "weak." And the word translated as "well" in the NIV is most often translated "saved." "Jesus came to seek out and to save the lost" (Lk. 19:10). The word *saved* is the same in both passages. I am certainly not suggesting that we should stop praying about sickness. (It is always right to pray for those in need.) I am simply suggesting that perhaps James was concerned about sickness of the soul more than sickness of the body. That would certainly fit with the passage to follow.

When One Has Sinned. When should we pray? We pray when we have sinned. Four-year-old Andrew made an honest mistake and spilled some milk. His mother responded in a screaming tirade. The little psychologist made an astute observation: "Mommy, you forgot to ask Jesus to help you be nice today, didn't you?"[13]

The most important prayers are those that acknowledge our sin. When an individual refuses to deal with sin through prayer, that person is in worse condition than when physically sick.

Some creative minds around the University of Southern Mississippi came up with a catchy slogan for their football team: "Let Us Prey." Clever play on words, isn't it? While some have taken offense at the slogan, it reminds us of a very important truth. When we fail to pray, we avail ourselves to become prey.

Peter couldn't watch and pray one hour in the Garden of Gethsemane, so he became prey for the Adversary. He later wrote, "Like a roaring lion your adversary the devil prowls around, looking for someone to devour...," or to "prey upon" (1 Pet. 5:8). It is true: We become prey when we don't pray.

How Should One Pray? (5:16b–17)

As a Person of Righteousness. The newspaper *The Indianapolis Star* carries a syndicated column by Billy Graham in which he answers spiritual questions from letters he has received. One such question asked this: "Do you have to be perfect before God will answer your prayers?" Mr. Graham answered, "Do young children have to be perfect before they can ask their father for something? No, of course not: if their father truly loves them, he wants them to come to him and share their wishes with him."[14] One need not be perfect to pray, but one must be righteous to be effective in prayer. The word *righteous* describes one whose desire and efforts are to do what it right in the eyes of God. He or she is not perfect, but earnestly desires to do what is right.

Stan Edmunds inspects houses for a living. On January 29, 2002, Edmunds was inspecting a property in Hinsdale, New Hampshire. The potential buyer and real estate agent were both present but in a different part of the house. Edmunds spotted a hidden shelf support. When he pulled on it, a drawer slid out. Inside were just some old papers—and four bank deposit bags. Edmunds unzipped a bag and found dozens of $100 bills. Immediately, he called the real estate agent and had him contact the family members of the most recent owner who was deceased. No one knew about the money, so no one would have known if Edmunds had filled his pockets. The grand total in the drawer was approximately $20,000. Stan Edmund's deed could be described as righteous; he did what was right even when it was costly.[15]

If you are living in an unrighteous manner, don't expect much from your prayer life. If you steal from your boss, lie to your friends, or cheat on your spouse, and then wonder why your prayers are not being answered, I would suggest that you study these verses again. No one is perfect; but prayer is only powerful when the one who is praying is also walking in the direction of righteousness.

As a Person of Faith. Verse 15, "The prayer of faith will save the sick, and the Lord will raise them up." What is a prayer offered in faith? According to 1 John 5:14, it is a prayer offered according to God's will. One could also say it is a prayer that is confident of God's will. How was it that the prophet Elijah could pray for no rain and God responded by withholding the rain? Do not think that Elijah was superhuman. He was ordinary, just like us. His prayer, however, was extraordinary (1 Kings 17–18). Elijah ministered to the Israelites who had turned away from God and forgotten the divine Word. Elijah, on the other hand, knew well what the scriptures taught. Moses had warned the people years before what would happen if they turned away from the Lord and began worshiping the idols of their pagan neighbors. God would shut up the heavens so that there would be no rain. Then the ground would not yield its fruit, and they would perish (Deut. 11:16, 17). Elijah prayed what he knew was the will of God. He also prayed specifically; there was no ambiguity about his request.

It is important to understand that one's faith may be more than strong enough, but the answer sought may not fit into the will of God. Faith is certainly a key, but it is not a guarantee. Three times the apostle Paul prayed that God would remove his "thorn in the flesh," whatever physical malady that may have been. Surely no one would accuse Paul of lacking faith, and yet, each time the answer was no, "my grace is sufficient for you" (2 Cor. 12:9). Consider Jesus in the garden of Gethsemane on the night before the cross. Surely no one would conclude that his faith was lacking! He prayed, "Father, if you are willing, remove this cup from me" (Lk. 22:42). God was not willing; the ultimate plan of salvation was at stake in that prayer. If Jesus, the Son of God, and Paul, the servant of God, both received "no" for an answer to their earnest prayers, then we should not be surprised that we too might be told "no" by God. God's will supercedes our faith, no matter how strong.

Does the possibility that God might answer our prayers by saying "no" lessen the power of prayer? To the contrary! It strengthens prayer's power. To know that God's perfect will guides the answers to our prayers means that whatever the answer, it is always in our best interest! God is a God of power; the Lord's creative genius reminds us of that truth. One hundred lightning bolts blast the earth every second. These eight million daily surges of power, traveling up to 90,000 miles per second, provide more energy than all of the electric generators in the United States combined. Even though three-quarters of the bolt's energy is used up in heat (the surrounding air heats up to 54,000 degrees Fahrenheit), enough energy remains to deliver a full 125 million volts of electricity.[16] All of that power cannot begin to compare to the power that is released when we pray.

What Should One Do While Praying? (5:19–20)

While you pray, you should keep on "doing." Just as James asserted that faith without deeds is dead, so prayer without action is also dead. Help others come to a true understanding of God. "Whoever turns a sinner from the error of his way will save him" (5:20, NIV). Prayer is never intended to be a substitute for a Christian's testimony in word or lifestyle. Thus, this last verse of James reminds us that praying for a lost sinner is the verbal part; touching the life of a lost sinner is the living part. Say your prayers, and live them, too!

Comparatively speaking, not many gain significance in this life. Even if one does, it is fleeting. Do you know what these names have in common: James Sherman, Charles Fairbanks, Thomas Marshall, Charles Dawes, Alben Barkley, Charles Curtis, John Nance Garner, and Henry Wallace? They were all Vice Presidents of the United States in the twentieth century. They are all but forgotten now, and yet, in their lives they each reached a pinnacle that few of us would dare to dream about. Earthly significance is fleeting, but saying and living one's prayers gives a disciple of Jesus eternal significance!

Chapter 1: Celebrating God in All Circumstances

[1] Judith Viorst, *Alexander and the Terrible, Horrible, No Good, Very Bad Day* (New York: Atheneum, 1972).

[2] Billy Graham, "Life's Mountains and Valleys," found on www.preachingtoday.com, a service of Christianity Today International and *Leadership Journal.*

[3] W. E. Vine, *Vine's Complete Expository Dictionary,* ed. Merrill F. Unger, William White, Jr. (Nashville: Nelson, 1996), 200.

[4] Bill White, "Payton Endures Repeated Blows," found on www. preachingtoday.com.

[5] Jill Briscoe, "Don't Waste the Pain," *Decision Magazine* 40, no. 11 (November, 1999): 42, cited on www. preachingtoday.com (January 2004).

[6] James Hardy Ropes, *A Critical and Exegetical Commentary on the Epistle of St. James* (Edinburgh: T.&T. Clark, 1916), 155.

[7] Author unknown, cited in Craig Massey, *Adjust or Self-Destruct* (Chicago: Moody Press, 1977), 17.

[8] Malcolm Gladwell, "The Trouble with Fries: Fast Food Is Killing Us. Can It Be fixed?" *The New Yorker* (5 March 2001), cited in Mark Galli, "Why Sin Tastes Good," on www.preachingtoday.com.

[9] Dietrich Bonhoeffer, *Temptation* (London: SCM Press, 1961), 33.

Chapter 2: Harnessing Our Life for God

[1] Edward Hersey Richards, "Wise Old Owl," from www.poetry-inspirational.org. Also cited in William J. Bennett, *The Moral Compass* (New York: Simon & Schuster, 1995), 152.

[2] Information obtained from http://www.cnn.com/2002/LAW/01/09/hockey.dad.trial/index.html.

[3] William Barclay, *The Letters of James and Peter,* The Daily Study Bible (Philadelphia: Westminster Press, 1960), 71.

[4] Quoted in James S. Hewett, ed., *Illustrations Unlimited* (Wheaton, Ill.: Tyndale, 1988), 475.

Chapter 3: Loving the Outcast

[1] Charles Colson, *Kingdom in Conflict* (Grand Rapids: Zondervan, 1987), 307.

[2] Dave Barry, *Dave Barry's Book of Bad Songs* (Kansas City, Mo.: Andrews MacNeel, 1997), quoted in Steve May, *The Story File* (Peabody, Mass.: Hendrickson, 2000), 199.

[3] Walter Knight, ed., *Knight's Master Book of New Illustrations* (Grand Rapids: Eerdmans, 1956), xx.

⁴James Rowe, "Love Lifted Me," copyright owner, John T. Benson, Jr.; renewed, 1940.

⁵"Judgmentalism Is Deadly to Human Relationship," *Record: Newsletter of Evangelicals Concerned* (Summer 1994): 1, as quoted in Leonard Sweet, *Carpe Mañana* (Grand Rapids: Zondervan, 2001), 24.

⁶*Seabiscuit,* prod. Gary Ross and Tobey Maguire, dir. Gary Ross, 129 min., Universal Studios, 2003, based on the book by Laura Hillenbrand (New York: Random House, 2001).

Chapter 4: Doing What You Believe

¹*Leadership Magazine* 4 (Summer 1983): 81.

²R. Kent Hughes, *James, Faith That Works* (Wheaton, Ill.: Crossway, 1991), 109.

³Elton Trueblood, "When Faith Becomes Practical," *Leadership Magazine* 11 (1989): 65, cited on www.preachingtoday.com.

⁴Donald W. McCullough, *The Trivialization of God* (Colorado Springs: NavPress, 1995), 13–14.

Chapter 5: Respecting the Danger of the Tongue

¹"To Illustrate," *Leadership Magazine* 17 (1996): 68.

²Herb Miller and Douglas V. Moore, *300 Seed Thoughts* (Lubbock, Tex.: Net Press, 1986), 52.

³"The Golden Age of Hymns," *Christian History* 31 (1991): 2, cited on www.preachingtoday.com.

⁴Author unknown, cited in Walter B. Knight, *Knight's Master Book of New Illustrations* (Grand Rapids: Eerdmans, 1973), 693.

Chapter 6: Living Wisely: Being God's Friend

¹Robert Frost, "The Road Not Taken," in *The Robert Frost Reader: Poetry & Prose,* ed. Edward Connery Latham (New York: Henry Holt, 2002), 60.

²R.Kent Hughes, *James, Faith That Works* (Wheaton, Ill.: Crossway, 1991), 155–56.

³"All in a Day's Work," *Readers Digest* 163 (October 2003): 57.

⁴Kevin Miller, "'Busted' Over Careless Words," obtained from www.preachingtoday.com.

⁵"Wisdom from Yogi Berra," *Parade Magazine* (December 26, 1996), cited in *Leadership Magazine* 17 (1996); quoted on www.preachingtoday.com.

⁶Roddy Chestnut, "Taming The Tongue," www.sermoncentral.com.

⁷Fred Rogers, "Mr. Rogers: Deep and Simple," *Christianity Today* (March 6, 2000):45, cited on www. preachingtoday.com.

⁸C.S. Lewis, *Mere Christianity* (New York: Macmilllan, 1952), 54.

Chapter 7: Warning against Insulting God

¹Richard J. Needham, "Speak the Truth," cited in *Quotable Quotes* (Pleasantville, N.Y.: Reader's Digest, 1997) 157.

²Dietrich Bonhoeffer, "Verbal Abuse," *Leadership Magazine* 2 (1980), cited on www.preachingtoday.com.

[3]President George W. Bush, "The Warsaw Speech," delivered June 15, 2001, found at Office of the Press Secretary, www.whitehouse.gov, http://www.whitehouse.gov/news/releases/2001/06/20010615-1.html.

[4]Bruce Felton and Mark Fowler, "Most Unusual Millionaire," in *The Best, Worst and Most Unusual,* ed. Felton and Fowler (New York: Galahad, 1976), 198–200.

[5]"Stupid Criminals," found on http://www.frontiernet.net/~viper1/stupid.html.

[6]"Vincent Van Gogh," Microsoft Encarta, 1997.

[7]Herb Miller and Douglas V. Moore, *300 Seed Thoughts* (Lubbock, Texas: Net Press, 1986), 99.

Chapter 8: Living Together in the Community of Faith

[1]Cicero, *Pro Balbo* 5:12.

[2]Cited in www.sermoncentral.com *Christian Character* January 2004.

[3]Ella Wheeler Wilcox, in *Quotable Quotes* (Pleasantville, N.Y.: Reader's Digest, 1997), 42.

[4]G. Braumann, *"Parakaleo," Dictionary of New Testament Theology* I, ed. Colin Brown (Grand Rapids: Zondervan, 1978), 569–71.

[5]Bonne Stefen, "Power of Positive Words," found on www.preachingtoday.com.

[6]Walter Elliot, in *Quotable Quotes,* 82.

[7]Robert Shannon, *1000 Windows* (Cincinnati: Standard, 1997), 186.

[8]"The Secret of Carl Lewis," found on www. preachingtoday.com.

[9]In R. Kent Hughes, *James, Faith That Works* (Wheaton, Ill.: Crossway, 1991), 243.

[10]John Cheever, "Disappointment in America," *Leadership* 17 (1996), cited on www.preachingtoday.com.

[11]Hughes, *James,* 253–54.

[12]Charles Swindoll, *James, Practical and Authentic Living* (Fullerton Calif.: Insight For Living, 1989), 189.

[13]Cathy Fussell, "Life in Our House," *Christian Parenting Today* (May/June 1991): 73.

[14]Billy Graham, "God answers us despite our imperfections," My Answer column, *Indianapolis Star,* 25 February 2002, E3. Distributed by Tribune Media Services.

[15]Rubel Shelly, "No Room for Crooks," found on www.HeartTouchers.com, 3/4/02.

[16]Edmund H. Harvey, Jr., *Reader's Digest Book of Facts* (Pleasantville, N.Y.: Reader's Digest, 1987), 367.

Printed in the United States
76250LV00002B/268-312

9 780827 229808